TREASURE HUNT

13 QUILTS INSPIRED BY ANTIQUE FINDS

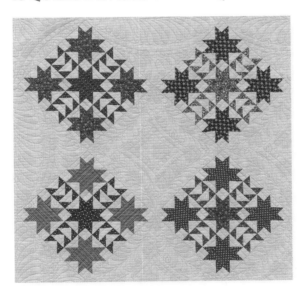

Linda Collins and Leah Zieber

Martingale®
Create with Confidence

Treasure Hunt: 13 Quilts Inspired by Antique Finds
© 2020 by Linda Collins and Leah Zieber

Martingale®
19021 120th Ave. NE, Ste. 102
Bothell, WA 98011-9511 USA
ShopMartingale.com

Printed in China
25 24 23 22 21 20   8 7 6 5 4 3 2 1

Library of Congress Cataloging-in-Publication Data
is available upon request.

ISBN: 978-1-68356-047-0

MISSION STATEMENT

We empower makers who use fabric and yarn
to make life more enjoyable.

CREDITS

**PUBLISHER AND
CHIEF VISIONARY OFFICER**
Jennifer Erbe Keltner

CONTENT DIRECTOR
Karen Costello Soltys

DESIGN MANAGER
Adrienne Smitke

MANAGING EDITOR
Tina Cook

PRODUCTION MANAGER
Regina Girard

ACQUISITIONS EDITOR
Karen M. Burns

INTERIOR DESIGNER
Angie Haupert Hoogensen

TECHNICAL EDITOR
Nancy Mahoney

PHOTOGRAPHER
Brent Kane

COPY EDITOR
Marcy Heffernan

ILLUSTRATOR
Sandy Loi

DEDICATIONS

*To all the quilters of the past who made the quilts that
inspire me to be a better quilter on a daily basis*
∼Linda

*To my dear family and wonderful friends who love and
support me with encouragement, critiques, and enthusiasm*
∼Leah

contents

Introduction 5
Treasure Hunting 6
Respect Your Antique Quilts 10

Projects
Cotillion 13
Mazurka 19
Quadrille 27
Turkey Trot 31
Polka 39
Square Dance 45
Virginia Reel 51
Gie Gordons 57
Minuet 63
Ladies' Chain 69
Two-Step 75
Waltz No. 2 79
Scottish Reel 87

About the Authors 94
Acknowledgments 96

INTRODUCTION

Our friendship began many years ago when we connected through an online quilt group. Since then, we have traveled between our two countries (Linda lives in Australia and Leah lives in the United States) to attend retreats and other quilting events, as well as to shop together and share our passion for antique quilts. We love to encourage and foster a passion for antique quilts with people from all around the world, and we share our enthusiasm for reproducing our quilts through teaching opportunities at home and abroad.

Our passion for antique quilts and related textiles has led to our collections that span more than 200 years of American, English, and French textile history, and we enjoy replicating our quilts using today's reproduction fabrics. We're always on the lookout for pieces that dance to their own tunes. Fun and unusual borders, dynamic settings, blocks we've never seen before, and exciting color combinations are all the elements that make us break into a happy dance.

Because we live in different countries and we can't always shop together, we are fortunate that today's technology allows us the luxury to call internationally for free and chat any time we need. Late nights and early mornings work best to accommodate the expansive time difference between us, so pajama-party video calls are the norm, as one of us is beginning and the other is ending the day. With coffee in hand and a bad case of bed head, we often come together to share our latest finds and pore over fabrics, books, and quilts.

Re-creating our own antique quilts is a passion we share with one another and now, thanks to Martingale, we're fortunate enough to share with you. The quilts we've selected include sizes small to large, with skill levels from easy to challenging. You can use your stash, your scraps, or the latest and greatest reproduction prints, but no matter what fabrics you use, we want you to make the quilts uniquely your own. We hope to inspire you with our antique quilts and encourage you with our reproductions so that you can fill your home with the beautiful history that is the patchwork quilt.

~Linda and Leah

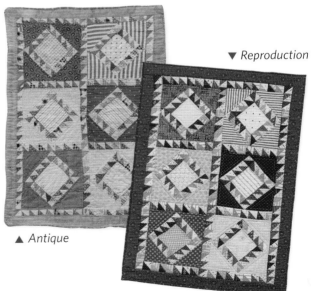

▼ *Reproduction*

▲ *Antique*

Treasure Hunting

Everyone always asks us, "Where did you find that quilt?" As antique-quilt collectors we spend a lot of time dancing our way through antique shops, flea markets, and quilt vendor booths. Navigating from town to town, one or the other of us is bound to shout, "Stop! There's an antique store!" Tires squealing, we pop a U-turn and head back to look for treasures. Some of our best quilts have been found in an obscure part of a small town, in a dark antique-mall booth, wadded up on the bottom shelf. Check out "Shopping Secrets" on page 8 for tips when shopping at antique stores.

Over the years we have come to know the most amazing vendors who sell at local and national quilt shows. These delightful people have helped and encouraged us with our collections. Getting to know them personally and developing a relationship over time has led to some fantastic quilt purchases, a few of which are featured in this book. Our vendor friends know our tastes and often go out of their way to locate quilts and other textiles within the scope of our collections. For this and many other reasons, we look forward to our visits each year. Get to know the quilt vendors at your local and national quilt and craft shows and let them know your interests. They just may have your perfect quilt. Always ask for their "best price" or if they can accommodate a layaway; remember, selling quilts is their business and they want you to be a return customer.

We also find antique and vintage quilts online at sites that are both auctions and retail shops. Always on the lookout for great finds, we'll give the other a heads-up on an auction item we think she'll love. Luckily, we don't collect *exactly* the same things. There are many websites that feature "live" online auctions from auction houses around the world, and great deals can be had. But, remember that your winning bid is not the bottom-line price. Auction houses usually add an additional percentage to the winning bid, and you'll still need to factor in the tax, shipping, handling, and currency conversions.

Opposite page, left: *We were pleased to find this gorgeous circa-1850s quilt at the Brimfield Antique Flea Market in 2017.* **Opposite page, right:** *Quilts on display are almost always for sale. Be sure to ask the vendor.*
This page, clockwise from top left: *Sometimes you hit it big and find tubs of quilts; more often it's just one quilt in a booth. Always examine the quilts fully on both sides. Flea markets are known for wide ranges in quilt styles, ages, and conditions. The quilts on display were seen at Brimfield in 2018.*

Take a friend when shopping. Having a second set of eyes is always a good idea when examining a quilt.

Calculate the full cost before you submit your bid. And be sure to check the item's condition—something that is always difficult to determine from photos and descriptions. Be prepared to ask for more information or additional photos to be sure of what you're purchasing. Don't wear out your wallet by competitive bid-dancing with another buyer; it's easy to get swept off your feet in the excitement of the live auction moment. Set your bid limit and be prepared to walk away when bidding goes beyond your price point.

We all have that favorite color, time period, or style that we look for in a quilt, and sometimes we can let our hearts run away with our wallets. When looking for the perfect purchase, pause and consider several key points before you buy. Condition is one of the most important aspects when collecting antique quilts. Those tagged museum quality in pristine condition will command higher prices, but they do make beautiful display pieces if your budget allows. Age does matter, and it is one of the determining factors in cost; earlier quilts and blocks typically

SHOPPING SECRETS

Finding your own fantastic antique quilts is sure to happen if you stick to some tried-and-true treasure-hunting techniques.

- *Before you hit the road, be sure to check the hours and days of operation on the places you want to visit; many have varied open and closed days and times.*

- *Check your maps and have a plan of approach for the day. Knowing how to get where you're going is key to saving time.*

- *Don't be shy when you walk through the door; friendly proprietors are always willing to offer the locations of the booths that may have quilts, so be sure to ask.*

- *Take the time to dig deep and look in boxes, drawers, trunks, and on the bottom shelves.*

- *Textiles are generally an afterthought for antique dealers and are often used for displays. Everything in the shop is usually for sale, even props, so ask if you can purchase any textiles that look like they may be part of a display. A dealer would often rather deconstruct part of their booth to get at a piece than miss out on a sale.*

- *Buyer beware! You'll see a lot of import fakes in the antique stores, so know what you're purchasing by doing your homework before you go. Read up on contemporary imports made to look like antiques and search every quilt you intend to buy for a manufacturer label. If it has one, it's not antique or vintage.*

- *Before you leave the store, remember to inquire as to other antique stores in the area. One of the best places to shop might just be a nearby home where a local is selling some of their own collections. Shop owners may be able to point you in the direction of other great places to find your treasures.*

command higher prices when other factors are equal. And quilts and blocks with provenance or signatures are some of the most sought-after in the collecting world, so be prepared to pay up for these. Keep in mind that you may not get back the full price of your purchase if you have to sell in a pinch. Quilt prices are unpredictable and subject to trends.

Don't automatically overlook the damaged quilt items. If you are just getting started with your collection, remember that blocks, tops, and quilt fragments can inspire through their color, design, and layout. An added bonus is that these damaged goods are often considerably less expensive than an intact quilt. Split, popped, or minimally stained fabric should be evaluated with an open mind, especially if using the piece as inspiration for a reproduction. Likewise, quilts with damaged backings or binding but undamaged fronts should be considered for purchase. They are typically less expensive and easily repaired. However, we always recommend avoiding mildewed textiles. Mold spores are not only dangerous allergens, but they require significant bleaching to eradicate, which usually results in damage to printed and colored textiles. Keeping that one caution in mind, don't skip the sale bins. Damaged goods offer great inspiration, and sometimes amazing deals can be had with items that require minimal repair.

This page, top: *Flea markets and antique shops can provide inspiration on displaying your treasures. Always ask before taking photos.* **This page, bottom:** *Be sure to look under all the layers of quilts hung on racks; sometimes the good stuff is folded underneath.*

respect your antique quilts

No matter where you find your treasures, it's important to treat them in a manner that both inspires today's collectors and quilters, and preserves them for future generations. By following a few simple tips, you will help ensure that your antique quilts maintain their beauty and provide many years of delight. Go ahead and incorporate your antique and reproduction quilts into your home decor; they are your treasures, and they should be enjoyed!

DISPLAYING YOUR QUILTS

Antique and reproduction quilts provide limitless possibilities for display. We often use our small quilts as table toppers or bundle them into side-table baskets. Frames and shadow boxes are perfect for individual quilt blocks and other smaller textile pieces. Try creating a wall mosaic of your small quilts along a hall or stairwell for a remarkable presentation. Larger quilts look fantastic on the backs of couches, quilt racks, or ladders. Even a simple stack of antique quilts placed on a shelf can create a wonderful design element in any room. Try layering your quilts in coordinating colors for a fantastic look on any bed.

Take care when displaying your damaged textiles. Quilts with fragile parts should not be hung or draped: it adds too much stress on the already worn or torn areas. Strategically fold your tattered quilts to show the best parts and hide the worn spots. These items can be stacked and displayed on shelves or on top of blanket chests for a nice visual appeal while minimizing further damage.

CARING FOR YOUR QUILTS

No matter how you display your quilts, there are some important tips that we practice to keep our textiles clean and free from damage. One of the most important elements to consider when displaying any textile is lighting. In order to maintain true colors, quilts require indirect lighting, so avoid settings next to windows or walls that receive direct sunlight or lamplight. Additionally, changing out your quilts with each of the four seasons and periodically refolding your stored and displayed quilts will ensure that no one quilt receives too much light over time. Years from now you'll be glad you put your quilts away in the closet for a few months, because they'll have maintained their genuine colors. Using sleeves instead of pins or nails when hanging quilts will also help to prevent tearing and allow the weight to be off the antique fabrics, thus minimizing damage over time.

We rarely wash our antique quilts, and there's an important reason why. Today's water is often treated with chlorine, fluoride, and other chemicals. These elements in the water can change the dye chemistry in printed textiles, particularly older ones, and the results can be drastic. Colors can severely fade and fabric can even disintegrate, so ask yourself if the dirt is significant enough to warrant the risk. You may want to leave it alone and find a creative way to display your item so the stain doesn't show. Or, try vacuuming your quilt with a hand vacuum if there's dust or surface dirt; this is often a better alternative than the washing machine. And, if your antique is particularly aromatic, but not in a good way, try airing it over a banister or outside on the clothesline. First drape the clothesline with a sheet, then lay your quilt over the line and cover with a second sheet. This double-draping method prevents soil from the clothesline or passing birds from further damaging the quilt. A few hours in a soft breeze can often reduce or even eliminate an offensive odor.

storing your quilts

Care should be taken when storing your antique textiles, particularly the cotton variety. Cedar chests are great for woolen items but toxic to cotton quilts—get them out! And never store your quilts directly on a wooden shelf, even if it's painted. A moisture barrier is essential to prevent the acids from leaching out of the wood and onto the fabric, leaving a stain. Evidence of this process is seen in older quilts where a yellow or darkish square stain appears in one area of the quilt where it sat on a wood surface. So, line the wood with a plain cloth or piece of waxed paper; this prevents the quilt fabric from touching the wood directly.

When your quilts are not on display, the best storage scenario is to put them in a clean, white cotton pillowcase and place them on a top shelf in a closet, keeping them off the floor in the event of a flood. The room should be dark and the shelf should be lined with a barrier such as waxed paper or plastic sheeting. Keep the closet light turned off when not in use. Never, ever seal your quilts in plastic tubs or plastic bags. This type of storage seals in moisture, causing mildew and odors to thrive. The result can be smelly quilts with black stains that are nearly impossible to remove.

Above right: *Hanging antique quilts on a quilt ladder lets you display multiple quilts at a time. Just be sure to refold them and rotate them periodically to prevent damage from sun and dust.* **Right:** *Stacking quilts is always a fun way to display your treasured possessions. Here, the stack is showcased in front of a quilt hanging on vintage shutters that are layered in front of an old fireplace surround to give depth and texture to the room.*

COTILLION

Cotillion offers the simplicity of the Nine Patch block in a stately layout that gives the impression of a more complicated design. Fanciful and fun, the light sashing within each block, as well as the sashing that separates the blocks, creates clear paths to the darker tones used for each nine-patch unit. Your invitation awaits; join in the excitement of re-ceating your own antique reproduction masterpiece.

MATERIALS

Yardage is based on 42"-wide fabric.

¼ yard *each* of 25 assorted dark prints in blues, browns, and grays for nine-patch units

¼ yard *each* of 26 assorted light and medium shirting prints for nine-patch units

1½ yards of microdot light shirting print for blocks

⅓ yard of pink check for blocks

⅛ yard of medium brown print for nine-patch units

2⅛ yards of light print for sashing strips

1¾ yards of double-pink print for sashing cornerstones, setting triangles, and binding

7⅓ yards of fabric for backing

88" × 88" piece of batting

CUTTING

All measurements include ¼"-wide seam allowances.

From *each* of the 25 assorted dark prints, cut:
• 2 strips, 1½" × 42" (50 total)
• 1 strip, 1½" × 21" (25 total)

From the remainder of 1 dark blue print, cut:
• 1 strip, 1½" × 21"

From *each* of the 26 assorted light or medium shirting prints, cut:
• 2 strips, 1½" × 42" (52 total); crosscut 1 of the strips into 2 strips, 1½" × 21" (52 total)

From the microdot light shirting print, cut:
• 30 strips, 1½" × 42"; crosscut into 324 rectangles, 1½" × 3½"
• 1 strip, 3½" × 42"

From the pink check, cut:
• 6 strips, 1½" × 42"; crosscut 4 of the strips into 100 squares, 1½" × 1½"

From the medium brown print, cut
• 2 strips, 1½" × 42"

From the light print for sashing, cut:
• 6 strips, 11½" × 42"; crosscut into 64 rectangles, 3½" × 11½"

From the double-pink print, cut:
• 3 strips, 3½" × 42"; crosscut into 24 squares, 3½" × 3½"
• 1 strip, 5½" × 42"; crosscut into 4 squares, 5½" × 5½". Cut each square into quarters diagonally to yield 16 sashing triangles.
• 2 strips, 9¾" × 42"; crosscut into 6 squares, 9¾" × 9¾". Cut each square into quarters diagonally to yield 24 side triangles.
• 2 squares, 8¾" × 8¾"; cut each square in half diagonally to yield 4 corner triangles
• 9 strips, 2" × 42"

REPLICATING THE ANTIQUE LOOK

We chose to use a mixed selection of nine-patch units to give the feel of the antique quilt. You could also use nine matching units to give your blocks a controlled scrappy look.

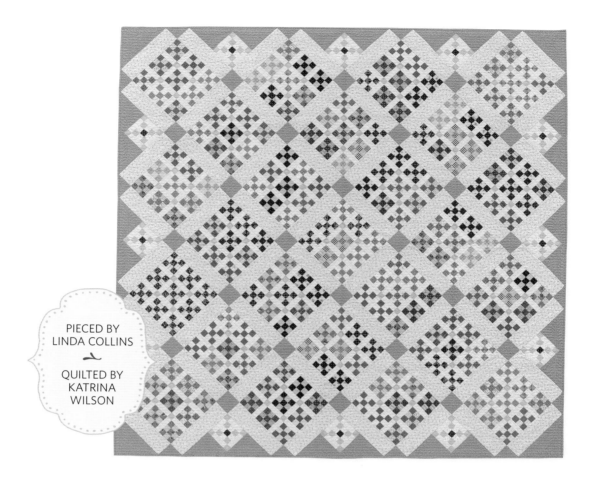

MAKING THE NINE-PATCH UNITS

Use ¼" seam allowances. Press the seam allowances in the directions indicated by the arrows.

1 Sew matching dark print 1½" × 42" strips to each long edge of a light or medium shirting print 1½" × 42" strip to make strip set A, which should measure 3½" × 42", including seam allowances. Crosscut the strip set into 18 A segments, 1½" × 3½".

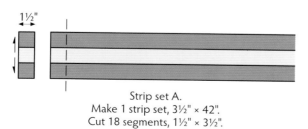

Strip set A.
Make 1 strip set, 3½" × 42".
Cut 18 segments, 1½" × 3½".

2 Using 1½" × 21" strips that match strip set A, sew shirting print strips to each long edge of a dark print strip to make strip set B, which should measure 3½" × 21", including seam allowances. Crosscut the strip set into nine B segments, 1½" × 3½".

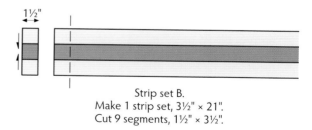

Strip set B.
Make 1 strip set, 3½" × 21".
Cut 9 segments, 1½" × 3½".

3 Sew two A segments and one B segment together to make a nine-patch unit measuring 3½" square, including the seam allowances. Repeat to make a total of nine units.

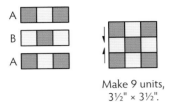

Make 9 units,
3½" × 3½".

4 Repeat steps 1–3 with the remaining dark print and light or medium shirting print strips to make a total of 225 nine-patch units.

MAKING THE BLOCKS

Lay out nine assorted units, 12 microdot 1½" × 3½" rectangles, and four pink check 1½" squares in five rows. Sew the pieces together into rows. Join the rows to make a block measuring 11½" square, including the seam allowances. Repeat to make a total of 25 blocks.

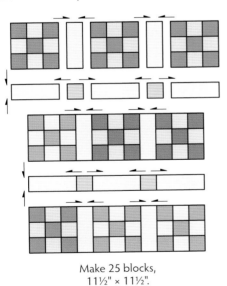

Make 25 blocks,
11½" × 11½".

Making the Pieced Side Triangles

1 Sew medium brown 1½" × 42" strips to each long edge of a light shirting print 1½" × 42" strip to make strip set C, which should measure 3½" × 42", including seam allowances. Crosscut the strip set into 24 C segments, 1½" × 3½".

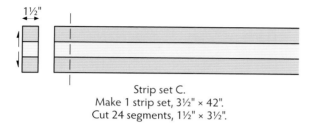

Strip set C.
Make 1 strip set, 3½" × 42".
Cut 24 segments, 1½" × 3½".

2 Sew light shirting print 1½" × 21" strips that match strip set C to each long edge of the dark blue 1½" × 21" strip to make strip set D, which should measure 3½" × 21", including seam allowances. Crosscut the strip set into 12 D segments, 1½" × 3½".

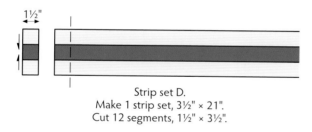

Strip set D.
Make 1 strip set, 3½" × 21".
Cut 12 segments, 1½" × 3½".

3 Join two C segments and one D segment to make a nine-patch unit measuring 3½" square, including seam allowances. Make 12 units.

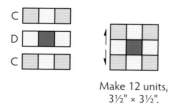

Make 12 units,
3½" × 3½".

4 Sew pink check 1½" × 42" strips to each long edge of the microdot 3½" × 42" strip to make strip set E, which should measure 5½" × 42", including seam allowances. Crosscut the strip set into 24 E segments, 1½" × 5½".

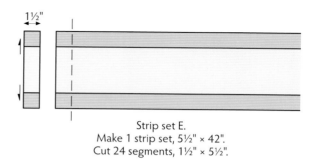

Strip set E.
Make 1 strip set, 5½" × 42".
Cut 24 segments, 1½" × 5½".

5 Sew microdot 1½" × 3½" rectangles to opposite sides of a nine-patch unit from step 3. Join E segments to the top and bottom of the unit. The unit should measure 5½" square, including seam allowances. Make 12 units.

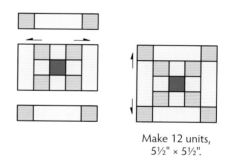

Make 12 units,
5½" × 5½".

6 Sew double-pink side triangles to adjacent sides of a unit from step 5 to make a pieced side triangle. Make 12.

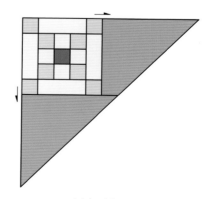

Make 12 units.

ASSEMBLING THE QUILT TOP

Lay out the blocks, light print 3½" × 11½" rectangles, double-pink 3½" squares, double-pink sashing triangles, pieced side triangles, and double-pink corner triangles in diagonal rows as shown in the quilt assembly diagram below. Sew the pieces together into rows. Join the rows, adding the corner triangles last. Trim and square up the quilt top, making sure to leave ¼" beyond the points of the sashing strips for seam allowances. The quilt top should measure 79¾" square.

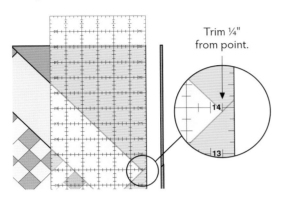

Trim ¼" from point.

FINISHING THE QUILT

For more information on finishing your quilt, visit ShopMartingale.com/HowtoQuilt.

1 Layer the quilt top, batting, and backing. Baste the layers together.

2 Quilt by hand or machine. The quilt shown is custom machine quilted with cross-hatching and a central wreath in the blocks, swirling wreaths in the sashing, and wreaths in the outer pink setting triangles.

3 Use the double-pink 2"-wide strips to make the binding, and then attach the binding to the quilt. Using a narrow binding helps create an authentic antique look.

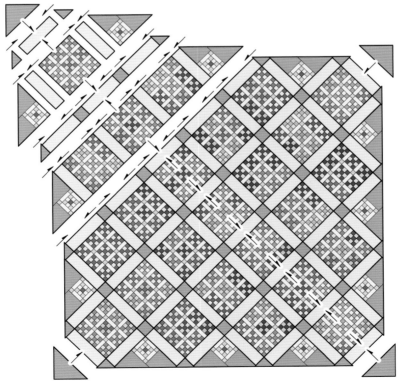

Quilt assembly

ANTIQUE INSPIRATION

A charming variation of a Double Nine Patch quilt, Cotillion was an online Etsy purchase and is believed to have come from the northeast Ohio area. It features many indigo and shirting prints from the 1880 to 1910 era. The fine cotton batting belies the quilt's age, and it is hand quilted in straight lines. Its neutral color choice and thin batting make it perfect as a summer quilt. ~Linda

Mazurka

FINISHED QUILT
57¼" × 57¼"

FINISHED BLOCK
9½" × 9½"

Half-square triangles delightfully dance around the red X of the Mazurka block and help to create the secondary nine-patch designs. The triple sashed borders of red and white boldly frame the blocks to set them apart and allow each one to sparkle splendidly on its own. Scrappy or controlled, color placement in the half-square triangles can help to create unique designs within each block.

Materials

Yardage is based on 42"-wide fabric. Fat eighths measure 9" × 21".

16 fat eighths of assorted medium and dark prints for blocks (referred to collectively as "dark")

2⅞ yards of white solid for blocks and sashing

¼ yard of green print for blocks

⅛ yard of orange print for blocks

⅝ yard of red print A for blocks

2 yards of red print B for sashing and binding

3⅝ yards of fabric for backing

64" × 64" piece of batting

Cutting

All measurements include ¼"-wide seam allowances.

From *each* of the dark prints, cut:
- 3 squares, 4" × 4" (48 total)

From the white solid, cut:
- 6 strips, 4" × 42"; crosscut into 48 squares, 4" × 4"
- 3 strips, 5½" × 42"; crosscut into 16 squares, 5½" × 5½". Cut the squares into quarters diagonally to yield 64 side triangles.
- 4 strips, 3¾" × 42"; crosscut into 32 squares, 3¾" × 3¾". Cut the squares in half diagonally to yield 64 corner triangles.
- 1 strip, 12½" × 42"; crosscut into 20 strips, 1¾" × 12½"
- 1 strip, 10" × 42"; crosscut into 20 strips, 1¾" × 10"
- 5 strips, 1¾" × 42"

From the green print, cut:
- 3 strips, 1½" × 42"; crosscut into 64 squares, 1½" × 1½"

From the orange print, cut:
- 1 strip, 2¼" × 42"; crosscut into 16 squares, 2¼" × 2¼"

From red print A, cut:
- 8 strips, 2¼" × 42"; crosscut into 64 rectangles, 2¼" × 4½"

From red print B, cut:
- 2 strips, 12½" × 42"; crosscut into 40 strips, 1¾" × 12½"
- 2 strips, 10" × 42"; crosscut into 40 strips, 1¾" × 10"
- 4 strips, 1¾" × 42"
- 6 strips, 2" × 42"

MAKING THE BLOCKS

Use ¼" seam allowances. Press seam allowances in the directions indicated by the arrows.

1 Draw a diagonal line from corner to corner in both directions to form an X on the wrong side of the white 4" squares. Layer a marked square on top of a dark square, right sides together. Sew ¼" from both sides of the drawn lines. Cut the units apart horizontally and vertically. Then cut the units apart on the drawn lines to yield eight half-square-triangle units. Trim the units to measure 1½" square, including seam allowances. Make 384 units.

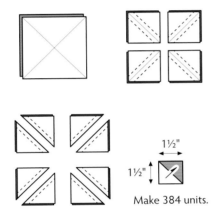

Make 384 units.

2 Join three units from step 1 in a vertical row to make a left unit, making sure the dark triangles are all oriented in the same direction. Using the same prints in the same order, join three triangles in a vertical row to make a right unit. Make four identical left units and four identical right units measuring 1½" × 3½", including seam allowances. Repeat to make 16 sets of four right and four left identical triangle units.

Make 64 of each unit, 1½" × 3½".

USE TRIANGLE PAPERS

If you prefer, you can use your favorite triangle papers for making eight-at-a-time 1" finished half-square-triangle units.

3 Sew a green square to the bottom of each right unit. The unit should measure 1½" × 4½", including seam allowances. Make 16 sets of four identical units (64 total).

Make 64 units, 1½" × 4½".

4 Sew a left unit to one short side of a white side triangle. Sew a matching right unit from step 3 to the other short side of the triangle. Make 16 sets of four identical side units (64 total).

Make 64 units.

5 Lay out four red A 2¼" × 4½" rectangles, four matching side units, one orange square, and four white corner triangles in diagonal rows. Sew the pieces together into rows. Join the rows, adding the corner triangles last to make a block measuring 10" square, including seam allowances. Make 16 blocks.

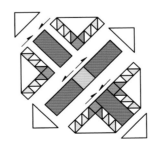

Make 16 blocks, 10" × 10".

PIECED BY
LINDA COLLINS

QUILTED BY
KATRINA
WILSON

MAKING THE PIECED SASHING

1 Sew red B 1¾" × 10" strips to opposite long edges of a white 1¾" × 10" strip to make a vertical sashing strip measuring 4¼" × 10", including seam allowances. Make 20 sashing strips.

Vertical sashing strip.
Make 20 strips,
4¼" × 10".

2 Sew red B 1¾" × 12½" strips to opposite long edges of a white 1¾" × 12½" strip to make a horizontal sashing strip measuring 4¼" × 12½", including seam allowances. Repeat to make a total of 20 sashing strips.

Horizontal sashing strip.
Make 20 strips,
4¼" × 12½".

3 Sew red B 1¾" × 42" strips to opposite long edges of a white 1¾" × 42" strip to make a strip set measuring 4¼" × 42", including seam allowances. Crosscut the strip set into 10 A segments, 1¾" × 4¼", including seam allowances.

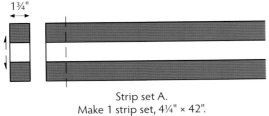

Strip set A.
Make 1 strip set, 4¼" × 42".
Cut 10 A segments, 1¾" × 4¼".

4 Sew white 1¾" × 42" strips to opposite long edges of a red B 1¾" × 42" strip to make a strip set measuring 4¼" × 42", including seam allowances. Make two strip sets. Crosscut the strip sets into 25 B segments, 1¾" × 4¼", including seam allowances.

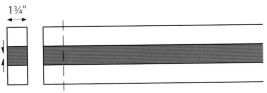

Strip set B.
Make 2 strip sets, 4¼" × 42".
Cut 25 B segments, 1¾" × 4¼".

ASSEMBLING THE QUILT TOP

1 Join two A segments, five B segments, and four horizontal sashing strips to make a sashing row measuring 4¼" × 57¼", including seam allowances. Make five sashing rows.

Make 5 rows, 4¼" × 57¼".

2 Join five vertical sashing strips and four blocks to make a block row measuring 10" × 57¼", including seam allowances. Make four block rows.

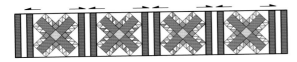

Make 4 rows, 10" × 57¼".

3 Join the sashing rows and block rows, alternating them as shown in the quilt assembly diagram below to complete the quilt top. The quilt top should measure 57¼" square.

FINISHING THE QUILT

For more information on finishing your quilt, visit ShopMartingale.com/HowtoQuilt.

1 Layer the quilt top, batting, and backing. Baste the layers together.

2 Quilt by hand or machine. The quilt shown is custom machine quilted with ditch stitching, plus straight lines and feathers in the blocks and sashings.

3 Use the red print B 2"-wide strips to make the binding, and then attach the binding to the quilt. Using a narrow binding helps create an authentic antique look.

Quilt assembly

ANTIQUE INSPIRATION

Houston International Quilt Festival is a fantastic place to find antique quilt vendors en masse. Be sure to visit them first upon your arrival and make your purchases early. Good buys and great quilts are usually the first to go, so don't hesitate if you find a favorite. I was lucky enough to be the first to spy this circa-1880 triple-sashed cross block quilt. It charmed me with its many early prints, so I latched on! I have found this beautiful quilt to be a real conversation starter whenever I bring it out to share.
~Linda

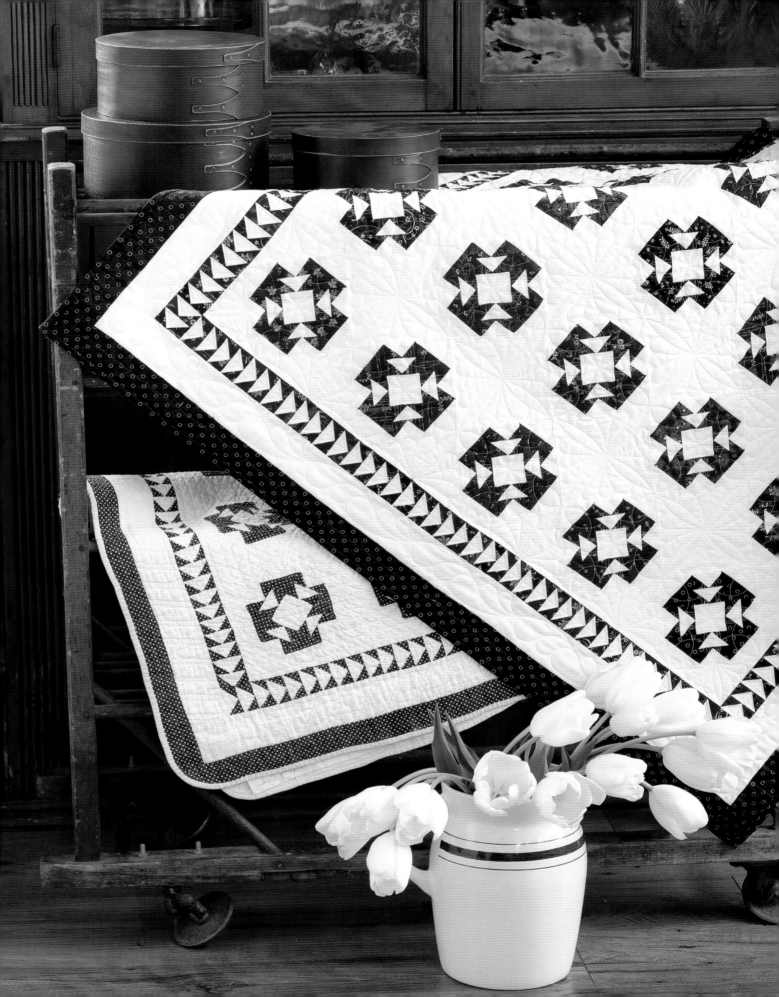

quadrille

FINISHED QUILT
42" × 42"
FINISHED BLOCK
4½" × 4½"

*Spying this classic gem from across the room will make any heart skip
a beat. Petite and lively, the little blue-and-white blocks dance in flawless rhythm
as an orchestra of geese surrounds the center. It's just right for a wall hanging
or table topper. Big on charm, this pretty patchwork treasure is reminiscent of
a bygone era when two-couple dances were the highlight of the dance floor.*

Materials

Yardage is based on 42"-wide fabric.

2 yards of ivory solid for blocks, setting squares
and triangles, and inner and middle borders

2 yards *total* of assorted navy prints for blocks,
inner and outer borders, and binding

2¾ yards of fabric for backing

48" × 48" piece of batting

Cutting

All measurements include ¼"-wide seam allowances.

From the ivory solid, cut:

• 2 strips, 5" × 42"; crosscut into 16 squares, 5" × 5"

• 4 squares, 7⅝" × 7⅝"; cut each square into quarters
diagonally to yield 16 side setting triangles

• 2 squares, 4⅛" × 4⅛"; cut each square in half
diagonal to yield 4 corner triangles

• 14 strips, 2" × 42"; crosscut into:
   25 squares, 2" × 2"
   376 rectangles, 1¼" × 2"

• 4 strips, 2⅜" × 42"; crosscut into 50 squares,
2⅜" × 2⅜"

• 4 strips, 2½" × 42"

From the assorted navy prints, cut:

• 4 strips, 2⅜" × 42"; crosscut into 50 squares,
2⅜" × 2⅜"

• 24 strips, 1¼" × 42"; crosscut into 752 squares,
1¼" × 1¼"

• 9 strips, 2" × 42"

Making the blocks

Use ¼" seam allowances. Press the seam allowances
in the directions indicated by the arrows.

1. Using a pencil, draw a diagonal line from corner
to corner on the wrong side of each navy 1¼"
square. Place a marked navy square on one end of an
ivory 1¼" × 2" rectangle, right sides together. Sew on
the drawn line. Trim off the corner, leaving a ¼" seam
allowance. Press. Repeat to add a second marked
square to the opposite end of the rectangle. Sew, trim,
and press as before to make a flying-geese unit
measuring 1¼" × 2", including the seam allowances.
Make 376 flying-geese units.

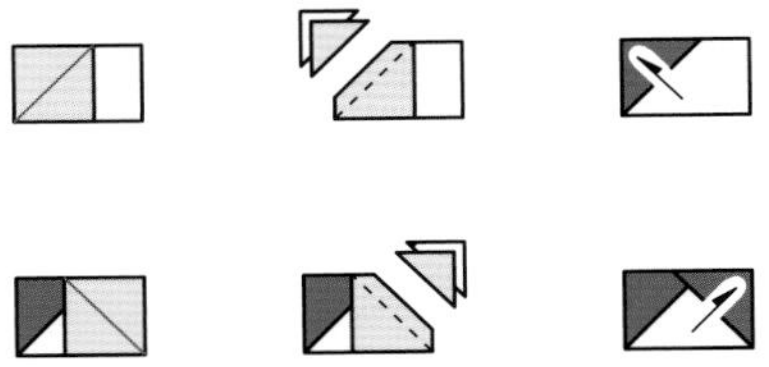

Make 376 units,
1¼" × 2".

ADDED DIMENSION

*The original circa-1890s quilt was made with only
two fabrics, one dark and one light, but we chose to
go scrappy with the darks used for the blocks.
Scrappiness gives added character to the charming
little Capital T blocks. Try making each with a
different blue print or mix the blue prints within
each block—both techniques will help carry the eye
and give depth and dimension to your reproduction.
Small- and medium-scale prints work best.*

PIECED BY
SUSAN GREENE

QUILTED BY
MERRY JO
REMBOLD

2 Draw a diagonal line from corner to corner on the wrong side of each ivory 2⅜" square. Layer a marked square right sides together with a navy 2⅜" square. Sew ¼" from each side of the marked line. Cut the unit apart on the marked line to make two half-square-triangle units measuring 2" square, including the seam allowances. Make 100 units.

Make 100 units,
2" × 2".

3 Join two flying-geese units to make a double flying-geese unit measuring 2" square, including seam allowances. Make 100 units. Set aside the remaining flying-geese units for the pieced border.

Make 100 units,
2" × 2".

4 Lay out four half-square-triangle units, four double flying-geese units, and one ivory 2" square in three rows. Sew the units together into rows. Join the rows to make a block measuring 5" square, including the seam allowances. Make 25 blocks.

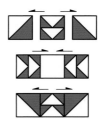

Make 25 blocks,
5" × 5".

ASSEMBLING THE QUILT TOP

1 Using the remaining flying-geese units, join 42 units to make an inner side border measuring 2" × 32", including the seam allowances. Repeat to

make a second inner side border. Join 46 flying-geese units in the same manner to make the top border, which should measure 2" × 35". Repeat to make the bottom border.

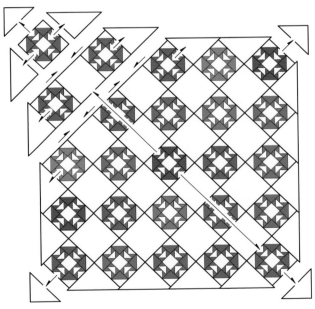

Make 2 side borders,
2" × 32".

Make 2 top/bottom borders,
2" × 35".

2 Referring to the quilt assembly diagram below, arrange the blocks and the ivory setting squares and triangles in diagonal rows. Sew the pieces together into rows. Join the rows, adding the corner triangles last. Trim and square up the quilt-top center, making sure to leave ¼" beyond all points for seam allowances. The quilt top should measure 32" square, including the seam allowances.

Quilt assembly

3 Sew the 32"-long flying-geese borders to opposite sides of the quilt top, paying careful attention to the direction the geese are flying. Add the 35"-long flying-geese borders to the top and bottom of the quilt.

4 Measure the quilt length through the center. Trim two ivory 2½"-wide strips to this measurement. Sew these strips to opposite sides of the quilt top. Measure the width of the quilt top through the center, including the borders just added. Trim the remaining two ivory 2½"-wide strips to this measurement. Sew these strips to the top and bottom of the quilt top.

5 Repeat step 4 using the navy 2"-wide strips, joining strips as necessary to achieve the required length. The quilt top should measure 42" square.

FINISHING THE QUILT

For more information on finishing your quilt, visit ShopMartingale.com/HowtoQuilt.

1 Layer the quilt top, batting, and backing. Baste the layers together.

2 Quilt by hand or machine. The quilt shown is custom machine quilted with loopy stars and feathers in the alternate blocks and middle border. The flying geese are stitched in the ditch.

3 Join the remaining navy 2"-wide strips end to end to make the binding, and then use it to bind the quilt. Using a narrow binding helps create an authentic antique look.

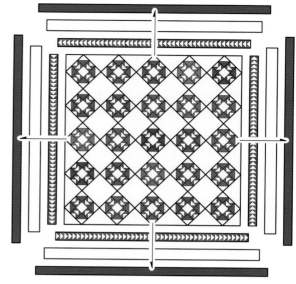

Adding borders

ANTIQUE INSPIRATION

Capital T is for temperance. This great little quilt dates to circa 1890s, when the temperance movement was popular and Prohibition was on the rise. Constructed of two different prints, the quilt's red-and-white shirting has faded to near white, while the stable indigo dye remains dark blue. Likely used for a child's crib or cot, this small-scale pattern would look equally great as a larger quilt. What a surprise to find this prize in a local hometown antique store. ~Leah

TurKey TroT

Lively and quick, Turkey Trot elevates the spirits to create a happy and heartwarming quilt. The rich, brown outer border balances the dark stars and alternate blocks, while the pink half-square-triangle inner border frames the center. Whether you piece it by hand or machine, this heirloom beauty will brighten up any room.

MaTerIaLs

Yardage is based on 42"-wide fabric.

⅜ yard of dark brown print for blocks

⅜ yard of black print for blocks

⅜ yard of green print for blocks

⅝ yard of pink print for blocks and inner border

1⅜ yards of white solid for blocks and inner border

1⅛ yards of medium brown print for setting squares and triangles

1⅞ yards of dark brown stripe for outer border

½ yard of light brown print for binding

3⅝ yards of fabric for backing

64" × 64" piece of batting

Transparent template plastic

Fine-tip permanent marker

cuTTIng

All measurements include ¼"-wide seam allowances. Before you begin cutting, refer to "Making and Using Templates" on page 33 for information on cutting the fabric pieces using the templates.

From the dark brown print, cut:
- 72 diamonds using template D

From the black print, cut:
- 72 diamonds using template D

From the green print, cut:
- 72 diamonds using template D

From the pink print, cut:
- 72 diamonds using template D
- 2 strips, 5" × 42"; crosscut into 15 squares, 5" × 5"

From the white solid, cut:
- 108 squares using template A
- 72 triangles using template B
- 36 rectangles using template C
- 2 strips, 5" × 42"; crosscut into 15 squares, 5" × 5"

From the medium brown print, cut:
- 2 strips, 10½" × 42"; crosscut into 4 squares, 10½" × 10½"
- 2 squares, 15½" × 15½"; cut the squares into quarters diagonally to yield 8 side triangles
- 2 squares, 8" × 8"; cut the squares in half diagonally to yield 4 corner triangles

From the *lengthwise* grain of the dark brown stripe, cut:
- 4 strips, 6½" × 60"

From the light brown print, cut:
- 7 strips, 2" × 42"

MAKING THE BLOCKS

Use ¼" seam allowances. These blocks were assembled by hand. Finger-press the seam allowances in the directions indicated by the arrows.

1. Pin two brown D diamonds right sides together. Start by pushing a pin through at one point of the diamond where the pencil lines meet, making sure to pin through the points on both pieces of fabric. Do the same on the other point. Keep the pins at right angles to the fabric. Repeat halfway along the seamline, making sure to pin through both stitching lines. Line up another pin with the one already in the diamond tip, angling it horizontally, and pin through both pieces of fabric. Remove the pin at a right angle. Repeat for the other diamond points and center. Doing this prevents the fabric from shifting when sewing.

HAND PIECING THE UNITS

When pinning the pieces, we like to use fine glass-head pins for accuracy. If you are unfamiliar with hand piecing, you can find many good hand-piecing tutorials online.

2. Using an unknotted thread and beginning at one corner, take a stitch, and then backstitch twice on the seamline. Make small, evenly spaced running stitches on the seamline, checking the reverse side and taking several small backstitches at the end. Do not stitch into the seam allowances. Trim the thread. Repeat the process to make a total of 36 diamond units.

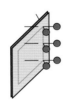

MAKING AND USING TEMPLATES

The rotary cutter has certainly been a great tool for speeding up our cutting over the years, but there are still occasions when a template provides more accurate results, such as for pieces with odd measurements not found on a rotary-cutting ruler. Follow these instructions to make your templates and use them to cut out the fabric pieces.

1. Trace the patterns A–D on page 37 onto transparent template plastic using a fine-tip permanent marker. Be sure to transfer the template letter and the grain-line arrow as well. Cut out each template exactly on the outer line.

2. Place the desired template face down on the wrong side of the appropriate fabric, aligning the grain-line arrow with the straight of grain. Trace around the template using a fine-lead pencil. Trace additional shapes from the same fabric in the same manner, positioning the shapes at least ½" apart. Always make sure that pieces on the outside edges of the block are cut on the straight grain. If possible, cut triangles so that a straight-grain edge meets a bias edge, giving the piece less chance of stretching while stitching.

3. Cut out each fabric piece, adding approximately a ¼" seam allowance on all sides. The seam allowance can be approximate, because you'll be stitching on the marked lines.

PIECED BY
ROBYN AHERN

QUILTED BY
KATRINA
WILSON

3 Sew the diamond units together in pairs to make 18 star halves, working from the outer edges to the center. Join two halves to make a star. Make nine stars.

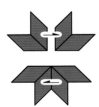
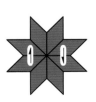

Make 9 stars.

4 Inset white A squares into the star points of a brown star. To inset, pin and stitch the first seam, working toward the inner corner, and backstitch at the end. Do not cut the thread. Pivot the pieces, then align and pin the second seam. Pass the needle through the seam allowances from the end of the first seam to the

start of the second seam, as needed. Stitch the second seam, backstitching at the beginning and end. Cut the thread. Make nine A units.

Unit A.
Make 9 units.

5 Lay out two black D diamonds, two green D diamonds, two pink D diamonds, two white B triangles, and one white A square. Begin with a black diamond and, working left to right, join the diamonds in the same way as before, ending with a black diamond. Repeat step 4 to inset two white triangles and one white square. Make 36 B units.

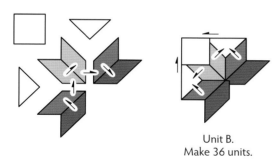

Unit B.
Make 36 units.

6 Join one A unit, four B units, and four white C rectangles in the same way as before to make a block measuring 10½" square, including seam allowances. Make nine blocks.

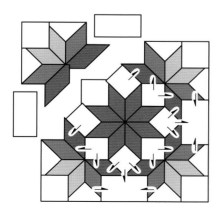

Make 9 blocks,
10½" × 10½".

MAKING THE PIECED BORDER

1 Draw a diagonal line from corner to corner in both directions to form an X on the wrong side of the white 5" squares. Layer a marked square on top of a pink square, right sides together. Sew ¼" from both sides of the drawn lines. Cut the units apart both horizontally and vertically. Then cut the units apart on the drawn lines to yield eight half-square-triangle units. Trim the units to measure 2" square, including seam allowances. Make 120 units (4 will be extra).

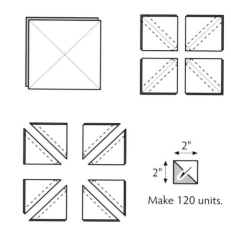

Make 120 units.

2 Join 28 half-square-triangle units to make a side border measuring 2" × 42½", including seam allowances. Repeat to make a second side border.

Make 2 side borders,
2" × 42½".

3 Join 30 half-square-triangle units to make a top border measuring 2" × 45½", including seam allowances. Repeat to make the bottom border.

Make 2 top/bottom borders,
2" × 45½".

USE TRIANGLE PAPERS

If you prefer, you can use your favorite papers for making eight-at-a-time 1½" finished half-square-triangle units.

If the border isn't a perfect fit, you'll need to adjust the seam allowance in a few places. To make the strip slightly longer, make a narrower seam allowance. If the border is a little bit too long, make a wider seam allowance. Be sure to spread the adjustments across the entire border, and it will work out just fine.

ASSEMBLING THE QUILT TOP

1 Lay out the blocks, medium brown 10½" squares, and medium brown side and corner triangles in diagonal rows as shown in the quilt assembly diagram below. Sew the pieces together into diagonal rows. Join the rows, adding the corner triangles last. Trim and square up the quilt-top center, making sure to leave ¼" beyond all points for seam allowances. The quilt center should measure 42⅞" square, including seam allowances.

Quilt assembly

2 Sew the pieced side borders to the quilt-top center, making sure to place the white triangles next to the quilt center. Sew the pieced top and bottom borders

to the quilt top, making sure to place the white triangles next to the quilt center. The quilt top should measure 45⅞" square, including seam allowances.

3 Sew the brown stripe 6½"-wide strips to the sides first, then to the top and bottom of the quilt top. Miter the corners. For more information on mitered borders, visit ShopMartingale.com/HowtoQuilt. The quilt top should measure 57⅞" square.

Adding borders

FINISHING THE QUILT

For more information on finishing your quilt, visit ShopMartingale.com/HowtoQuilt.

1 Layer the quilt top, batting, and backing. Baste the layers together.

2 Quilt by hand or machine. The quilt shown is custom machine quilted with ditch stitching and straight lines in the blocks, feathers in the setting squares, straight lines in the pieced border, and feathers in the outer border.

3 Use the light brown 2"-wide strips to make the binding, and then attach the binding to the quilt. Using a narrow binding helps create an authentic antique look.

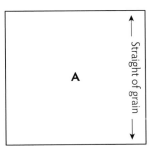

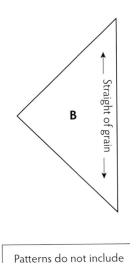

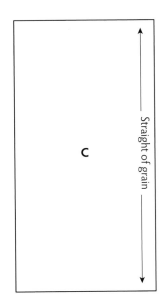

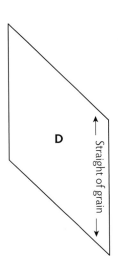

Patterns do not include seam allowances.

ANTIQUE INSPIRATION

I was fortunate enough to snap up this charming quilt from an antique-quilt vendor at one of my annual Quilts in the Barn exhibits. Circa 1880s, its dark tones and striking Snow Crystal block make it a perfect winter display. ～*Linda*

POLKa

FINISHED QUILT
27½" × 24½"
FINISHED BLOCK
6" × 6¾"

Finding ways to incorporate antique and vintage blocks into something new is always fun. These antique flea-market-find blocks quickly danced together to be the star of the table. The geometric shape of the equilateral triangles makes for limitless layouts, so create your own design by setting the blocks any way you like!

Materials

Yardage is based on 42"-wide fabric.

½ yard *total* of 12 assorted prints in medium brown, dark brown, and dark blue for blocks (referred to collectively as "dark")

⅜ yard *total* of 12 assorted prints in light pink, medium pink, light brown, light blue, and light shirting for blocks (referred to collectively as "light")

⅝ yard of cream print for setting triangles and binding

⅞ yard of fabric for backing

29" × 32" piece of batting

Transparent template plastic

Fine-tip permanent marker

MAKING THE TEMPLATES

Follow these instructions to make the templates and use them to cut out the fabric pieces.

1 Trace the small and large triangle patterns on page 43 onto transparent template plastic using a fine-tip permanent marker. Be sure to transfer the grain-line arrow as well. Cut out each template exactly on the outer line.

2 Place the desired template face down on the wrong side of the appropriate fabric, aligning the grain-line arrow with the straight of grain. Trace around the template using a fine-lead pencil. Trace additional shapes from the same fabric in the same manner, positioning the shapes at least ½" apart.

3 Cut out each fabric piece.

CUTTING

All measurements include ¼"-wide seam allowances. Before you begin cutting, refer to "Making the Templates" on page 39 for information on cutting the fabric pieces using the templates.

From *each* of the assorted dark prints, cut:
- 6 triangles using the small triangle template (72 total)

From *each* of the assorted light prints, cut:
- 3 triangles using the small triangle template (36 total)

From the cream print, cut:
- 2 strips, 7" × 42"; cut 12 triangles using the large triangle template
- 3 strips, 1¼" × 42"

MAKING THE BLOCKS

Use ¼" seam allowances. Press seam allowances in the directions indicated by the arrows.

1 Select one set of six matching dark triangles and one set of three matching light triangles.

2 Arrange and sew the triangles together into rows, making sure the straight of grain is always at the top or bottom of the triangle. Join the rows to make a block measuring 6½" tall and 7¼" wide at the base. Make 12 blocks.

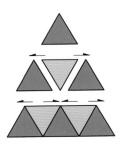
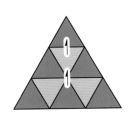

Make 12 blocks, 7¼" × 6½".

ANTIQUE INSPIRATION

Everyone always asks what to do with antique quilt blocks. If they're in good condition, add a bit of antique or reproduction fabric and make something useful. These circa-1880 blocks were a lucky find at the Brimfield Antique Flea Market, and there were more than enough to create a few small projects. The pyramid pattern allowed for limitless options while exploring different designs. Don't pass up an opportunity to combine the past and the present with a bunch of old blocks from your local flea market. ～*Linda*

PIECED AND
QUILTED BY
LINDA
COLLINS

ASSEMBLING THE QUILT TOP

1 Lay out the blocks in four rows as shown in the quilt assembly diagram at right. Place the cream triangles around the outer edges, making sure the straight of grain is at the top or bottom of the triangle.

2 Sew the blocks and triangles together into rows. Join the rows. The quilt top should measure 27½" × 24½".

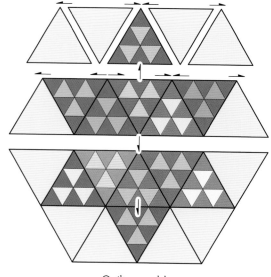

Quilt assembly

FINISHING THE QUILT

For more information on finishing your quilt, visit ShopMartingale.com/HowtoQuilt.

1 Layer the quilt top, batting, and backing. Baste the layers together.

2 Quilt by hand or machine. The quilt shown is machine quilted ¼" from each seamline.

3 Use the cream 1¼"-wide strips to make single-fold binding, and then attach the binding to the quilt. Using a narrow binding helps create an authentic antique look.

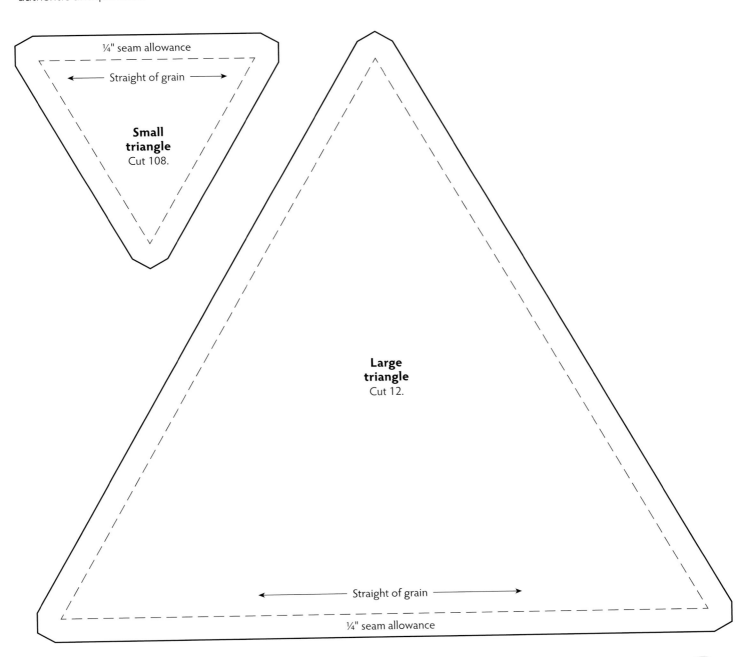

¼" seam allowance

← Straight of grain →

Small triangle
Cut 108.

Large triangle
Cut 12.

← Straight of grain →

¼" seam allowance

square dance

This unique little quilt looks so modern for its age. Your options are unlimited when it comes to color choices, but keeping all the values on the lighter side is sure to brighten your room. Perfect for a table topper or your favorite little baby, Square Dance can set your imagination free as you quickly dance strips into squares.

materials

Yardage is based on 42"-wide fabric. Materials here are given as lettered pairs of dark and light prints working from the center of the quilt outward.

⅝ yard of dark print (A1) for quilt top and binding

¼ yard of light print (A2) for quilt top

¼ yard *each* of dark print (B1) and light print (B2) for quilt top

½ yard *each* of dark print (C1) and light print (C2) for quilt top

¾ yard *each* of dark print (D1) and light print (D2) for quilt top

2½ yards of fabric for backing

46" × 46" piece of batting

cutting

All measurements include ¼"-wide seam allowances.

From fabric A1, cut:
- 7 strips, 2" × 42"
- 3 strips, 1½" × 42"

From fabric A2, cut:
- 5 strips, 1½" × 42"

From fabric B1, cut:
- 4 strips, 1½" × 42"

From fabric B2, cut:
- 3 strips, 1½" × 42"

From fabric C1, cut:
- 10 strips, 1½" × 42"

From fabric C2, cut:
- 10 strips, 1½" × 42"

From fabric D1, cut:
- 16 strips, 1½" × 42"

From fabric D2, cut:
- 14 strips, 1½" × 42"

FABRIC SELECTION

Choices abound when selecting fabrics for this great little quilt. We chose both prints and plaids for an authentic late nineteenth-century look.

making the strip sets

Use ¼" seam allowances. Press the seam allowances in the directions indicated by the arrows.

1 Using the A1 and A2 strips, sew the strips together along their long edges, alternating the colors and starting and ending with the 2"-wide A1 strips, to make strip set A. The strip set should measure 10½" × 42", including seam allowances. Set aside the remaining A2 strip.

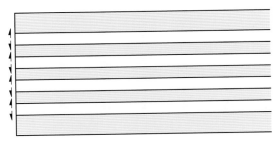

Strip set A.
Make 1 strip set,
10½" × 42".

45

2 Join the B1 and B2 strips, alternating the fabrics, to make strip set B, which should measure 7½" × 42", including seam allowances. In the same manner, sew the C1 and C2 strips together to make strip set C. Make two C strip sets measuring 10½" × 42", including seam allowances. Use the D1 and D2 strips to make strip set D. Make two D strip sets measuring 14½" × 42", including seam allowances. Set aside the remaining two D1 strips.

Strip set B.
Make 1 strip set,
7½" × 42".

Strip set C.
Make 2 strip sets,
10½" × 42".

Strip set D.
Make 2 strip sets,
14½" × 42".

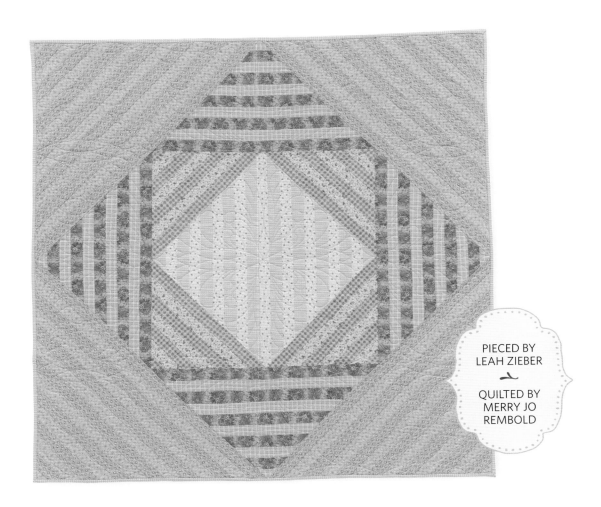

CUTTING THE TRIANGLES

1 Using a rotary cutter and a ruler marked with a 45° line, trim one end of the A strip set at a 45° angle. Rotate the strip set, align the edge of the ruler with the newly cut edge, and line up the 45° line with a seamline. (Do not align the ruler with the outer edge of the strip set.) Cut along the edge of the ruler to release the triangle as shown. Repeat to cut a second *identical* triangle. Set aside the leftover strip set for future projects.

2 Trim off ½" from each of the two triangles from step 1. Trim the A1 strip on the longest side of the triangle *only*. This is an important step and ensures the center square is the correct size.

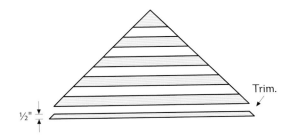

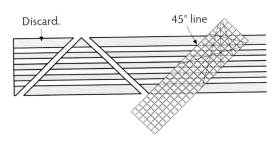

3 Repeat step 1 to cut four *identical* triangles from strip set B. From each C strip set, cut two *identical* triangles that have the darker strip on the longest side of the triangle. You will not use the triangles that have the lightest strip on the long side of the triangle. The leftover triangles and strip sets can be saved for future projects. Lay strip set D on your cutting mat with the *dark* strip at the bottom. Cut one triangle as described in step 1. Repeat to cut one triangle from the other D strip set.

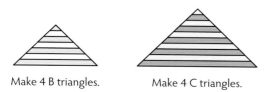

Make 4 B triangles.   Make 4 C triangles.

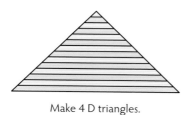

Make 4 D triangles.

4 Sew a leftover dark D1 strip to the light strip at the *top* of each D strip set. Align the 45° line with a seamline and trim the added strip even with the 45° edge. On the end closest to the 45° angle, carefully remove about 1" of stitching along the dark strip at the *bottom* of the strip set. Pin the end of the strip out of the way so that it doesn't interfere with the next step.

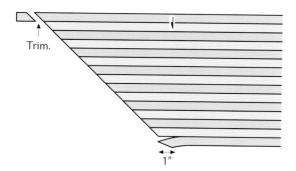

Trim.

1"

5 With the pinned strip at the bottom, align the 45° line on a ruler with a seamline and cut along the ruler to release the triangle. In the same way, cut a triangle from the remaining D strip set. You should have four *identical* triangles with the dark strip on the longest side and light tips. Set aside the remaining strip sets for future projects.

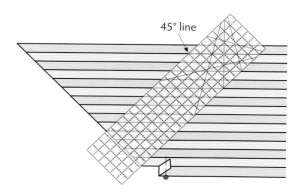

45° line

ASSEMBLING THE QUILT TOP

1 Sew the remaining 1½"-wide A2 strip between the two A triangles to make the center square. Trim the center square to measure 14" square, including seam allowances.

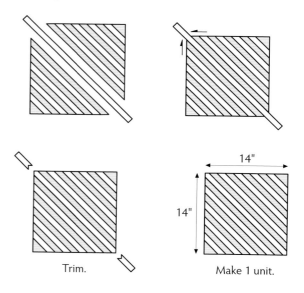

Trim.

14"

14"

Make 1 unit.

2 Sew B triangles to opposite sides of the center square. Sew B triangles to the two remaining sides. The quilt top should measure 20¼" square, including seam allowances.

Make 1 unit,
20¼" × 20¼".

3 Sew C triangles to opposite sides of the quilt top. Then sew C triangles to the two remaining sides. The quilt top should now measure 28½" square, including seam allowances.

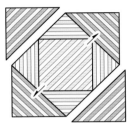 

Make 1 unit,
28½" × 28½".

4 Sew D triangles to opposite sides of the quilt top. Then sew D triangles to the two remaining sides to complete the quilt top. The quilt top should measure 40" square.

Quilt assembly

ANTIQUE INSPIRATION

Plaid, plaid, and more plaid—this unusual antique quilt dates to the turn of the 20th century and may have been made from shirt remnants. Unlike the reproduction, the antique quilt's strips are all foundation pieced onto a single piece of backing muslin, which causes the center to bow. With no batting or quilting, this little gem was likely used as a summer spread for a child's cradle or cot. ~Leah

FINISHING THE QUILT

For more information on finishing your quilt, visit ShopMartingale.com/HowtoQuilt.

1 Layer the quilt top, batting, and backing. Baste the layers together.

2 Quilt by hand or machine. The quilt shown is custom machine quilted with a large feather design in the center square and scallopy feathers in each of the quarter-square triangles.

3 Use the remaining 2"-wide A1 strips to make the binding, and then attach the binding to the quilt. Using a narrow binding helps create an authentic antique look.

virginia reel

FINISHED QUILT
15¾" × 21¾"
FINISHED BLOCK
5¼" × 5¼"

Two by two, the little blocks dance between half-square triangles and come together in this tiny cradle quilt—a perfect piece for the top of a small side table. For an authentic look, let the colors fall where they will and feel free to stray from convention—no need to stress over perfect points on your half-square triangles.

materials

Yardage is based on 42"-wide fabric.

½ yard *total* of 15 assorted light shirting prints for blocks and sashing

⅜ yard *total* of 15 assorted medium to dark shirting prints in reds, greens, blues, and blacks for blocks and sashing (referred to collectively as "dark")

4" × 8" rectangle *each* of red, blue, and black prints for blocks

⅛ yard of blue print for outer border

⅛ yard of red print for single-fold binding

⅝ yard of fabric for backing

20" × 26" piece of batting (optional; see "Pillowcase Method" on page 55)

cutting

All measurements include ¼"-wide seam allowances.

From *each* of the light shirting prints, cut:
- 2 squares, 3¼" × 3¼" (30 total)

From the remainder of the assorted light shirting prints, cut a *total* of:
- 6 squares, 2¾" × 2¾"
- 3 pairs of matching squares, 3½" × 3½" (6 total); cut the squares in half diagonally to yield 12 triangles

From *each* of the assorted dark shirting prints, cut:
- 2 squares, 3¼" × 3¼" (30 total)

From *each* of the red, blue, and black print rectangles, cut:
- 2 squares, 3½" × 3½"; cut the squares in half diagonally to yield 12 triangles

From the blue print, cut:
- 2 strips, 1¾" × 19¼"
- 2 strips, 1¾" × 15¾"

From the red print, cut:
- 3 strips, 1¼" × 42"

NOT-SO-POINTY POINTS

Antique cradle and doll quilts were often used as learning tools to teach young children to sew. Made in a hurry or made by a child with limited sewing skills, squared-off points were common, as were unequal half-square triangles. Half-square triangles cut from a 1¼" square can be stretchy, and thus challenging to work with and hard to keep accurate. But don't stress. Missed points and partial units are all part of the charm for this little quilt—leave it wonky, relax, and have fun!

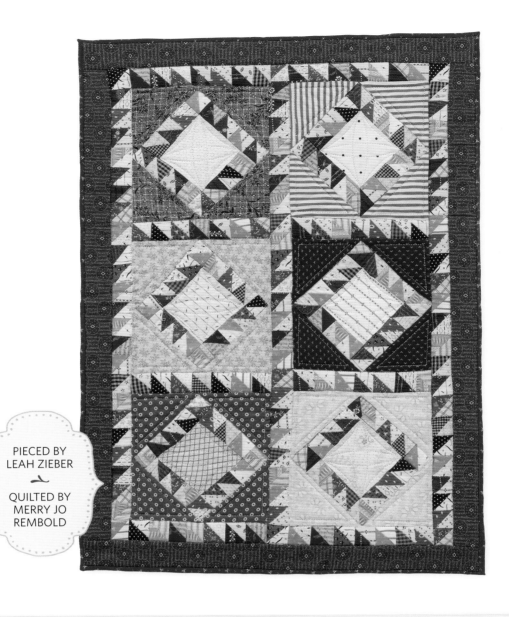

PIECED BY
LEAH ZIEBER

~

QUILTED BY
MERRY JO
REMBOLD

MAKING THE BLOCKS

Use ¼" seam allowances. Press seam allowances in the directions indicated by the arrows.

1 Draw a diagonal line from corner to corner in both directions to form an X on the wrong side of the light 3¼" squares. Layer a marked square on top of a dark square, right sides together. Sew ¼" from both sides of the drawn lines. Cut the units apart horizontally and vertically. Then cut the units apart on the drawn lines to yield eight half-square-triangle units. Trim each unit to 1¼" square, including seam allowances. Make 240 units.

1¼"

1¼"

Make 240 units.

Make sure to mix and match your fabrics for added variety. Scrappy is the way to go here!

2 Join three half-square-triangle units, making sure the dark triangles are all oriented in the same direction. The unit should measure 1¼" × 2¾", including seam allowances. Make 12 units.

Make 12 units,
1¼" × 2¾".

3 Join five half-square-triangle units, making sure the dark triangles are all oriented in the same direction. The unit should measure 1¼" × 4¼", including seam allowances. Make 12 units.

Make 12 units,
1¼" × 4¼".

4 Sew units from step 2 to the top and bottom of a light 2¾" square, positioning the dark triangles adjacent to the light square. Sew units from step 3 to opposite sides of the unit to make a block center measuring 4¼" square, including seam allowances. Make six units.

Make 6 units,
4¼" × 4¼".

5 Join matching light triangles to opposite sides of a center unit. Join matching light triangles to the remaining sides of the unit. Trim and square up the block to measure 5¾" square, including seam allowances. Make three light and three dark blocks.

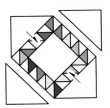

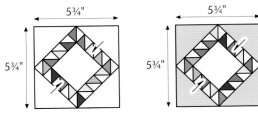

Make 3 of each block.

MAKING THE SASHING

1 Join seven half-square-triangle units, making sure the dark triangles are all oriented in the same direction, to make a horizontal sashing strip. The strip should measure 1¼" × 5¾", including seam allowances. Make eight strips.

Make 8 strips,
1¼" × 5¾".

2 Join 25 half-square-triangle units, making sure the dark triangles are all oriented in the same direction, to make a vertical sashing strip. The strip should measure 1¼" × 19¼", including seam allowances. Make three strips. You'll have 13 half-square-triangle units left over for your scrap box.

Make 3 strips,
1¼" × 19¼".

ANTIQUE INSPIRATION

Often the rarest treasures are found tattered and worn, living among the junk. This circa-1890s antique quilt was part of an auction lot of textiles that had nothing to do with quilts. Thank goodness no one else bid. Though worn and very faded, this endearing little cradle or doll quilt provided the perfect inspiration for a reproduction. ～*Leah*

To prevent the small half-square-triangle units from slipping as they pass through the feed dogs, be sure to insert pins at least every other seam. Pressing the sashing strips after adding each unit provides insurance that the strip will lie flat.

ASSEMBLING THE QUILT TOP

1 Lay out the blocks and horizontal sashing strips in two vertical rows, alternating the light and dark blocks as shown in the quilt assembly diagram below. Join the blocks and sashing strips to make the two columns measuring 5¾" × 19¼", including seam allowances.

2 Join the columns and vertical sashing strips to complete the quilt center. The quilt center should measure 13¼" × 19¼", including seam allowances.

3 Sew the blue 1¾" × 19¼" strips to opposite sides of the quilt center. Sew the blue 1¾" × 15¾" strips to the top and bottom of the quilt. The quilt top should measure 15¾" × 21¾".

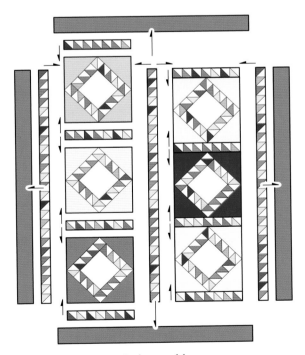

Quilt assembly

FINISHING THE QUILT

For more information on finishing your quilt, visit ShopMartingale.com/HowtoQuilt.

1 This quilt can be finished in the pillowcase method with no batting, like the original little quilt (see "Pillowcase Method" below). For a more modern finish, layer the quilt top with batting and backing, then baste the layers together.

2 Quilt by hand or machine. The quilt shown is machine quilted with an orange-peel variation in the block centers and outlines in the block triangles.

3 Use the red 1¼"-wide strips to make single-fold binding, and then attach the binding to the quilt. Using a narrow binding helps create an authentic antique look.

PILLOWCASE METHOD

Looking for a quick and simple finish? Omit batting and complete your little quilt with the pillowcase method. Cut backing fabric the same size as the quilt top. Layer the quilt top and backing, right sides together. Pin around the outer edges.

Machine stitch a scant ¼" seam allowance all the way around the edges of the quilt, making sure to stitch through both layers and leaving a 2" opening at one end for turning.

Turn the quilt right side out. Press flat and turn the opening seam allowances to the inside. Stitch the opening closed by hand or machine.

Gie Gordons

Lots of open space for fancy quilting sets the Gie Gordons blocks on a toe-tapping frolic through the cream background. This two-color quilt can be made scrappy using the same color in different prints throughout, or keep it simple with only one dark print. The on-point, alternate-block layout easily lends itself to enlarging for bigger bed coverings.

Materials

Yardage is based on 42"-wide fabric.

¼ yard *each* of 9 assorted red prints for blocks

3⅞ yards of cream print for blocks, setting squares and triangles, border, and binding

3⅓ yards of fabric for backing

59" × 59" piece of batting

Cutting

All measurements include ¼"-wide seam allowances.

From *each* of the red prints, cut:
- 3 strips, 1½" × 42"; crosscut into 64 squares, 1½" × 1½" (576 total)
- 1 strip, 2½" × 42"; crosscut into 5 squares, 2½" × 2½" (45 total)

From the cream print, cut:
- 1 strip, 10½" × 42"; crosscut into 3 squares, 10½" × 10½"
- 12 strips, 2½" × 42"; crosscut into 288 rectangles, 1½" × 2½"
- 6 strips, 2" × 42"
- 6 strips, 1½" × 42"; crosscut into 144 squares, 1½" × 1½"
- 2 squares, 8" × 8"; cut the squares in half diagonally to yield 4 corner triangles

From the *lengthwise* grain of the remaining cream print, cut:
- 2 strips, 5½" × 45"
- 2 strips, 5½" × 55"
- 2 squares, 15½" × 15½"; cut the squares into quarters diagonally to yield 8 side triangles
- 1 square, 10½" × 10½"

BLOCK SPECIFICS

To reflect the tonal quality of Gie Gordons, the instructions allow for each red print to appear in two blocks, once in the center star and flying-geese units and once in the four corner stars. This quilt would look equally wonderful, however, going completely scrappy or using just two prints.

PIECED BY
LINDA COLLINS

QUILTED BY
KATRINA
WILSON

MAKING THE BLOCKS

Use ¼" seam allowances. Press seam allowances in the directions indicated by the arrows.

1 Draw a diagonal line from corner to corner on the wrong side of each red 1½" square. Place a marked red square on one end of a cream 1½" × 2½" rectangle, right sides together. Sew on the marked line. Trim the excess corner fabric, ¼" from the stitched line. Place a marked square on the opposite end of the cream rectangle. Sew and trim as before

to make a flying-geese unit measuring 1½" × 2½", including seam allowances. Make nine sets of 32 matching units (288 total).

Make 288 units,
1½" × 2½".

2 Join four matching flying-geese units to make a side unit measuring 2½" × 4½", including seam allowances. Make nine sets of four matching units (36 total).

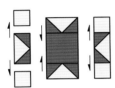

Make 36 units,
2½" × 4½".

3 Lay out four matching flying-geese units, four cream 1½" squares, and one red 2½" square that matches the flying-geese units in three rows. Sew the units together into rows. Join the rows to make a star unit measuring 4½" square, including seam allowances. Make nine sets of four matching units (36 total).

Make 36 units,
4½" × 4½".

4 Arrange four matching star units, four matching side units from a different red print, and one red 2½" square that matches the flying-geese units in three rows. Sew the pieces together into rows. Join the rows to make a block measuring 10½" square, including seam allowances. Make nine blocks.

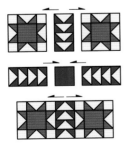

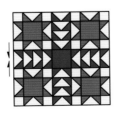

Make 9 blocks,
10½" × 10½".

last. Trim and square up the quilt top, making sure to leave ¼" beyond the points of all blocks for seam allowances. The quilt center should measure 43" square.

Quilt assembly

2 Measure the quilt top through the center from top to bottom. Trim the cream 5½" × 45" strips to this measurement and sew them to opposite sides of the quilt center.

3 Measure the quilt top through the center from side to side, including the borders just added, and then trim the cream 5½" × 55" strips to this measurement. Sew these strips to the top and bottom of the quilt. The quilt top should measure 53" square.

FINISHING THE QUILT

For more information on finishing your quilt, visit ShopMartingale.com/HowtoQuilt.

1 Layer the quilt top, batting, and backing. Baste the layers together.

2 Quilt by hand or machine. The quilt shown is custom machine quilted with cross-hatching in the blocks, square feather wreaths in the setting blocks and triangles, and feathering in the outer border.

3 Use the cream 2"-wide strips to make the binding, and then attach the binding to the quilt. Using a narrow binding helps create an authentic antique look.

ASSEMBLING THE QUILT TOP

1 Lay out the blocks, cream 10½" squares, and cream side and corner triangles in diagonal rows as shown in the quilt assembly diagram above right. Sew the blocks, squares, and side triangles in rows. Join the rows, adding the corner triangles

ANTIQUE INSPIRATION

The simplicity of a two-color quilt is easy on the eye and always captures the heart. This circa-1900s double-pink charmer was an irresistible eBay find that I couldn't pass up. Elevating the two fabrics into a very special quilt, the maker added her hand-quilting skills to give depth and beauty with extensive feathers in the alternate blocks and crosshatched diamonds in the borders. We took the reproduction to an even higher level by incorporating multiple red prints in the blocks. ~*Linda*

MINUET

FINISHED QUILT
53¼" × 59½"
FINISHED BLOCK
4½" × 4½"

Diminutive blocks take on a soft, elegant look when pieced in golden hues and framed with a toile border. Formal or fun, make the design your own by choosing your favorite color. Regardless of color choice, use small-scale prints to suit the scale of the blocks.

MATERIALS

Yardage is based on 42"-wide fabric unless otherwise specified.

⅛ yard *each* of 14 assorted butterscotch prints for blocks

½ yard *each* of 7 assorted cream prints for blocks, setting squares, and setting triangles

⅝ yard of butterscotch check for inner border and binding

2 yards of 54"-wide butterscotch toile for outer border

3⅓ yards of fabric for backing

60" × 66" piece of batting

CUTTING

All measurements include ¼"-wide seam allowances.

From *each* of the assorted butterscotch prints, cut:
- 2 strips, 1⅛" × 42"; crosscut into 48 squares, 1⅛" × 1⅛" (672 total)
- 1 strip, 1⅛" × 42"; crosscut into 3 strips, 1⅛" × 12" (42 total)

From *each* of the assorted cream prints, cut:
- 2 strips, 1¾" × 42"; crosscut into 24 squares, 1¾" × 1¾" (168 total)
- 2 strips, 1⅛" × 42"; crosscut into 6 strips, 1⅛" × 12" (42 total)
- 6 squares, 2½" × 2½" (42 total)

From the remainder of the assorted cream prints, cut a *total* of:
- 6 squares, 7¾" × 7¾"; cut the squares into quarters diagonally to yield 24 side triangles (2 will be extra)
- 30 squares, 5" × 5"
- 2 squares, 4¼" × 4¼"; cut the squares in half diagonally to yield 4 corner triangles

From the butterscotch check, cut:
- 6 strips, 2" × 42"
- 5 strips, 1¼" × 42"

From the *crosswise* grain of the butterscotch toile, cut:
- 2 strips, 7" × 54"

From the *lengthwise* grain of the butterscotch toile, cut:
- 2 strips, 7" × 50"

For your quilt to reflect the tonal quality of Minuet, you will use each cream print in six blocks and each butterscotch print in three blocks.

MAKING THE BLOCKS

Use ¼" seam allowances. Press seam allowances in the directions indicated by the arrows. For each block, select one cream 2½" square, four cream 1¾" squares, and one cream 1⅛" × 12" strip, all matching. You'll also need one butterscotch 1⅛" × 12" strip and 16 butterscotch 1⅛" squares, all matching. Repeat to make 42 blocks.

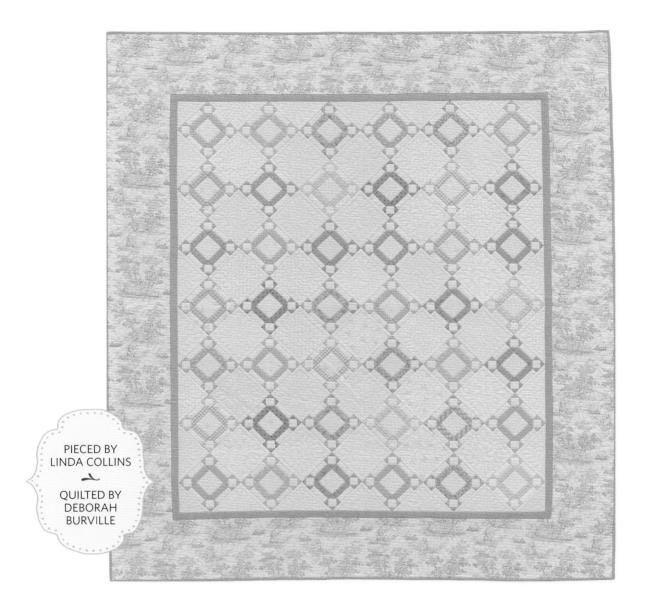

PIECED BY
LINDA COLLINS

QUILTED BY
DEBORAH
BURVILLE

1 Draw a diagonal line from corner to corner on the wrong side of four matching butterscotch 1⅛" squares. Place marked squares on opposite corners of a cream 1¾" square, right sides together and corners aligned. Sew on the marked line. Trim the excess corner fabric, leaving a ¼" seam allowance. In the same way, sew marked squares on the two remaining

corners of the cream square to make a corner unit measuring 1¾" square, including seam allowances. Make four matching corner units.

Make 4 matching units,
1¾" × 1¾".

2 Sew cream and butterscotch 1⅛" × 12" strips together to make a strip set measuring 1¾" × 12", including seam allowances. Cut the strip set into four side units measuring 1¾" × 2½", including seam allowances.

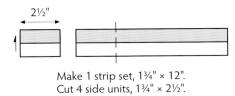

Make 1 strip set, 1¾" × 12".
Cut 4 side units, 1¾" × 2½".

3 Lay out the four corner units, four side units, and one cream 2½" square in three rows, rotating the units as shown. Sew the units together into rows. Join the rows to make a block measuring 5" square, including seam allowances. Make 42 blocks.

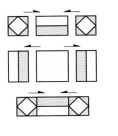

Make 42 blocks,
5" × 5".

ASSEMBLING THE QUILT TOP

1 Lay out the blocks and cream 5" squares in diagonal rows as shown in the quilt assembly diagram below. Place the cream side and corner triangles around the perimeter. Sew the blocks together into diagonal rows. Join the rows, adding the corner triangles last. Trim and square up the quilt top, making sure to leave ¼" beyond the points of all blocks for seam allowances. The quilt-top center should measure 38¾" × 45".

2 Join the butterscotch check 1¼"-wide strips end to end. Measure the length of the quilt top through the center from top to bottom. Cut two strips to this measurement and sew them to opposite sides of the quilt center.

3 Measure the quilt top through the center from side to side, including the borders just added, and cut two strips to this measurement. Sew these strips to the top and bottom of the quilt. The quilt top should measure 40¼" × 46½", including seam allowances.

4 For the butterscotch toile outer borders, measure the length of the quilt top through the center from

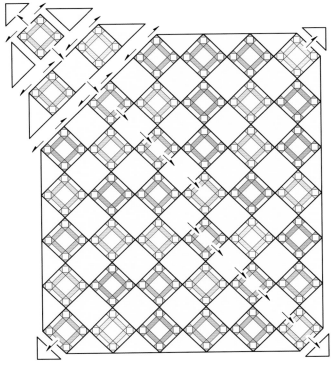

Quilt assembly

top to bottom. Trim the two 50"-long strips to this measurement. Sew the strips to opposite sides of the quilt top, making sure the design in both strips is going in the same direction.

5 Measure the quilt top through the center from side to side, including the borders just added, and trim the butterscotch toile 54"-long strips to this measurement. Sew these strips to the top and bottom of the quilt, again making sure the design in all the strips is going in the same direction. The quilt top should measure 53¼" × 59½".

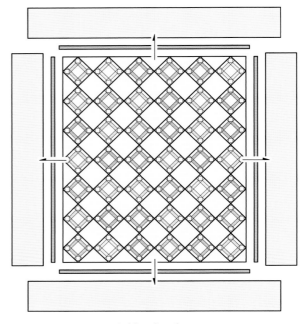

Adding borders

FINISHING THE QUILT

For more information on finishing your quilt, visit ShopMartingale.com/HowtoQuilt.

1 Layer the quilt top, batting, and backing. Baste the layers together.

2 Quilt by hand or machine. The quilt shown is custom machine quilted with ditch stitching in the blocks, feather wreaths in the block centers and the setting blocks, and triangles and feathers in the outer border.

3 Use the butterscotch check 2"-wide strips to make the binding, and then attach the binding to the quilt. Using a narrow binding helps create an authentic antique look.

ANTIQUE INSPIRATION

Red-and-white quilts are very collectible, so pick them up when you can, especially if the price is right. This circa-1900 beauty features a diminutive Rolling Stone block set with plain alternate blocks that create the perfect backdrop for a master quilter. The ¼"-spaced hand-quilted crosshatching is magnificent and reminiscent of much earlier quilts from the 19th century. This wonderful piece was purchased at Houston International Quilt Festival from a longtime friend and dealer. ~Linda

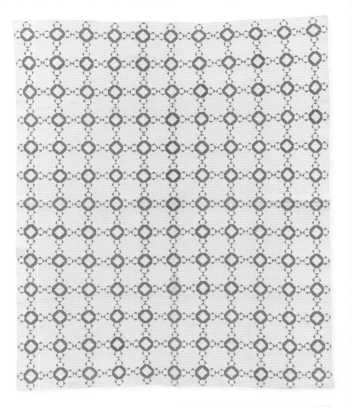

Ladies' Chain

Listen closely and you just might hear fiddles playing a lively background tune for our Ladies' Chain. And just like the Scottish country folk dance, our chain blocks keep the eye moving across the quilt. These wonderfully simple and easy-to-assemble blocks leave wide-open spaces for your whirly, twirly quilting. Keeping to three colors allows the accent to be on the chain and the quilting designs to be the focus.

Materials

Yardage is based on 42"-wide fabric.

4 yards of red print for blocks and borders

1¼ yards of light print for blocks

2⅞ yards of blue print for sashing, borders, and binding

7¼ yards of fabric for backing

86" × 86" piece of batting

Cutting

All measurements include ¼"-wide seam allowances.

From the red print, cut:
- 9 strips, 4¼" × 42"; crosscut into 73 squares, 4¼" × 4¼"
- 30 strips, 3" × 42"; crosscut *23 of the strips* into:
  36 strips, 3" × 13"
  36 rectangles, 3" × 8"
  36 squares, 3" × 3"

From the light print, cut:
- 9 strips, 4¼" × 42"; crosscut into 73 squares, 4¼" × 4¼"

From the blue print, cut:
- 6 strips, 5½" × 42"; crosscut into 12 rectangles, 5½" × 18"
- 14 strips, 3" × 42"
- 9 strips, 2" × 42"

Making the Blocks

Use ¼" seam allowances. Press seam allowances in the directions indicated by the arrows.

1 Draw a diagonal line from corner to corner in both directions to form an X on the wrong side of the light squares. Layer a marked square on top of a red 4¼" square, right sides together. Sew ¼" from both sides of the drawn lines. Cut the units apart horizontally and vertically. Then cut the units apart on the drawn lines to yield eight half-square-triangle units. The units should measure 1¾" square, including seam allowances. Make 584 units (4 units are extra).

1¾"
1¾"

Make 584 units.

TRIANGLE PAPERS

If you prefer, you can use your favorite papers for making eight-at-a-time 1¼" finished half-square-triangle units.

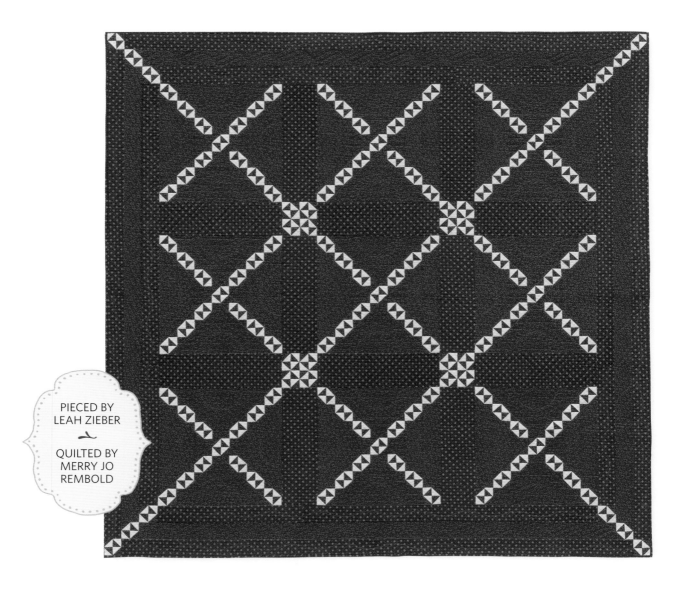

2 Arrange four half-square-triangle units in two rows of two units each. Sew the units together into rows. Join the rows to make a chain unit measuring 3" square, including seam allowances. Make 145 units. Set aside 28 units to use when assembling the quilt.

Make 145 units,
3" × 3".

3 Lay out five chain units and four red 3" squares in three rows, making sure to orient the units as shown. Sew the units together into rows. Join the rows to make a center unit measuring 8" square, including seam allowances. Make nine units.

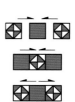

Make 9 units,
8" × 8".

4 Lay out one center unit, four chain units, and four red 3" × 8" rectangles, making sure to orient the units as shown. Sew the pieces together into rows. Join the rows to make a block unit measuring 13" square, including seam allowances. Make nine units.

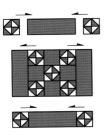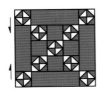
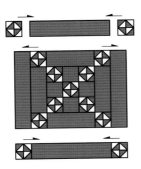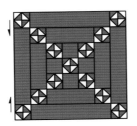

Make 9 units,
13" × 13".

5 Lay out one block unit, four chain units, and four red 3" × 13" rectangles, making sure to orient the units as shown. Sew the pieces together into rows. Join the rows to make a block measuring 18" square, including seam allowances. Make nine blocks.

Make 9 blocks,
18" × 18".

ASSEMBLING THE QUILT TOP

1 Arrange four chain units in two rows of two units each. Sew units together into rows. Join the rows to make a sashing cornerstone measuring 5½" square, including seam allowances. Make four cornerstones.

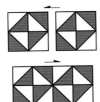

Make 4 cornerstones,
5½" × 5½".

2 Join three blocks and two blue 5½" × 18" rectangles to make a block row measuring 18" × 63", including seam allowances. Make three rows.

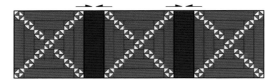

Make 3 rows,
18" × 63".

3 Join three blue 5½" × 18" rectangles and two sashing cornerstones to make a sashing row measuring 5½" × 63", including seam allowances. Make two rows.

Make 2 rows,
5½" × 63".

4 Join the blocks rows and sashing rows, alternating them as shown in the quilt assembly diagram on page 73, to make the quilt-top center. The quilt center should measure 63" square, including seam allowances.

5 Join the blue 3"-wide strips end to end. From the pieced strip, cut four 63"-long strips and four 73"-long strips.

6 Sew blue 63"-long strips to opposite sides of the quilt top. Sew a chain unit to each end of each remaining blue 63"-long strip, making sure to orient the units with a light triangle in the outer corner. Sew these strips to the top and bottom of the quilt top. The quilt top should measure 68" square, including seam allowances.

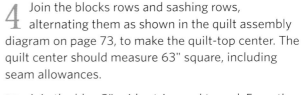

ANTIQUE INSPIRATION

Gifts from strangers can be endearing treasures. Following a quilt lecture, one of the guild members brought over her quilt and said, "None of my family members want this quilt and I know *you* will care and use it in your lectures. I would like you to have it." This statement made taking possession of the circa-1880s quilt very touching indeed. Little did the owner know her quilt would wind up featured in a book one day. The big open spaces of red and blue contrast with the small hourglass blocks to form a unique, timeless design that is easily re-created in any color or fabric combination. ～*Leah*

7 Join the remaining seven red 3"-wide strips end to end. From the pieced strip, cut four 68"-long strips. Sew two of the strips to opposite sides of the quilt top. Sew a chain unit to each end of each remaining red strip, making sure to orient the units with a light triangle in the outer corner. Sew these strips to the top and bottom of the quilt top. The quilt top should measure 73" square, including seam allowances.

8 Sew blue 73"-long strips from step 5 to opposite sides of the quilt top. Sew a chain unit to each end of each remaining blue strip, making sure to orient the units with a light triangle in the outer corner. Sew these strips to the top and bottom of the quilt top. The quilt top should now measure 78" square.

FINISHING THE QUILT

For more information on finishing your quilt, visit ShopMartingale.com/HowtoQuilt.

1 Layer the quilt top, batting, and backing. Baste the layers together.

2 Quilt by hand or machine. The quilt shown is custom machine quilted in the ditch around the Chain blocks to make them pop. The wide blue sashing is quilted with crosshatching. The red areas are quilted with feather half-wreaths and the borders are quilted with feathers and a wavy cable.

3 Use the blue 2"-wide strips to make the binding, and then attach the binding to the quilt. Using a narrow binding helps create an antique look.

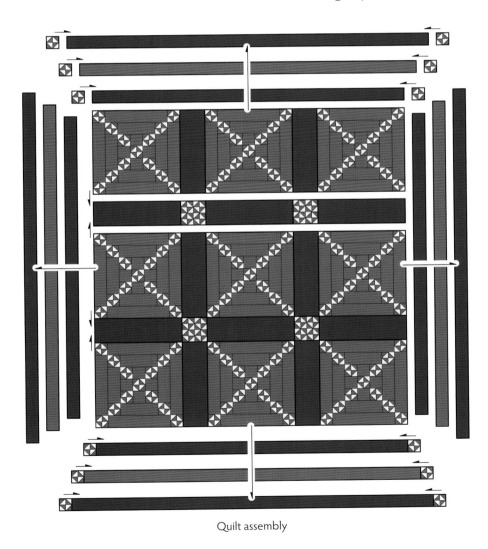

Quilt assembly

TWO-STEP

FINISHED QUILT
48½" × 60½"
FINISHED BLOCK
12" × 12"

Like the two-step country dance, this classic country quilt is both fun and easy. This project comes together quickly to deliver big appeal for every generation. Reproduction prints, bright prints, florals, or batiks—all work well for this time-honored pattern. Use your favorites and have fun "dancing" the two-step.

MATERIALS

Yardage is based on 42"-wide fabric.

¼ yard *total* of assorted stripes for block centers

2⅝ yards *total* of assorted light prints for blocks

2 yards *total* of assorted dark prints for blocks

⅜ yard of red print for binding

3⅛ yards of fabric for backing

55" × 67" piece of batting

SCRAP-BAG BUSTER

Courthouse Steps quilts are a variation on the Log Cabin and have been made in America for over 150 years. We've stayed true to antique colors by selecting shirting prints for the lights, and rich browns, reds, purples, and greens for the darks. As in the original, adding an outer light strip to the blocks causes the dark areas of the quilt to float. The small strip sizes in Two-Step allow you to use those leftover scraps you've been saving. Imagine a quilt filled with all your favorite fabrics!

CUTTING

All measurements include ¼"-wide seam allowances.

From the assorted stripes, cut:
- 20 rectangles, 2" × 3½" (A; ensure the stripe runs lengthwise on the long side)

From the assorted light prints, cut:
- 40 rectangles, 1¼" × 3½" (B)
- 40 rectangles, 1¼" × 5" (D)
- 40 rectangles, 1¼" × 6½" (F)
- 40 rectangles, 1¼" × 8" (H)
- 40 rectangles, 1¼" × 9½" (J)
- 40 rectangles, 1¼" × 11" (L)
- 40 rectangles, 1¼" × 12½" (N)

From the assorted dark prints, cut:
- 40 rectangles, 1¼" × 3½" (C)
- 40 rectangles, 1¼" × 5" (E)
- 40 rectangles, 1¼" × 6½" (G)
- 40 rectangles, 1¼" × 8" (I)
- 40 rectangles, 1¼" × 9½" (K)
- 40 rectangles, 1¼" × 11" (M)

From the red print, cut:
- 6 strips, 2" × 42"

MAKING THE BLOCKS

Use ¼" seam allowances. Press seam allowances in the directions indicated by the arrows.

1. Sew light B rectangles to opposite sides of a striped A rectangle to make a unit measuring 3½" square, including seam allowances. Make 20 units.

Make 20 units,
3½" × 3½".

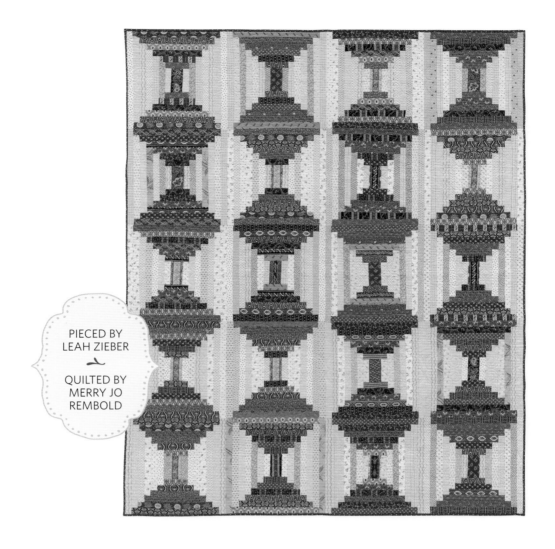

PIECED BY
LEAH ZIEBER

~

QUILTED BY
MERRY JO
REMBOLD

2 Sew dark C rectangles to the top and bottom of a
unit from step 1 to make a center unit measuring
3½" × 5", including seam allowances. Make 20 units.

3 Repeat steps 1 and 2, adding the D–N rectangles
to make a block measuring 12½" square,
including seam allowances. Make 20 blocks.

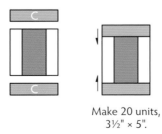

Make 20 units,
3½" × 5".

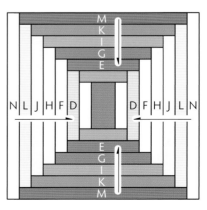

Make 20 blocks,
12½" × 12½".

AUTHENTIC LOOK

For a scrappy and authentic antique look, vary print positions throughout the blocks to keep the eye dancing between the steps. You can achieve this by cutting the same fabric in varying strip sizes to ensure different placement within the blocks.

ASSEMBLING THE QUILT TOP

Lay out the blocks in five rows of four blocks each as shown in the quilt assembly diagram below, making sure the same prints are not placed next to each other. Sew the blocks together into rows. Join the rows to complete the quilt top. The quilt top should measure 48½" × 60½".

Quilt assembly

FINISHING THE QUILT

For more information on finishing your quilt, visit ShopMartingale.com/HowtoQuilt.

1 Layer the quilt top, batting, and backing. Baste the layers together.

2 Quilt by hand or machine. The original antique quilt had no batting and was foundation pieced by hand. We chose to make this quilt using modern techniques. The simplicity of the pattern allows for a more complex quilting design. The quilt shown is custom machine quilted using a square scroll design, set on point, in the dark areas and a similar scroll design in the light areas.

3 Use the red 2"-wide strips to make the binding, and then attach the binding to the quilt. Using a narrow binding helps create an authentic antique look and ensures the outer logs will show the full width of ¾".

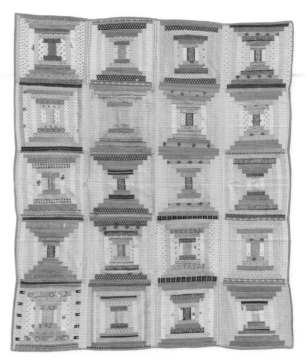

ANTIQUE INSPIRATION

One of the best pieces of advice for bidding at online auctions is to set your maximum price bid and walk away. When you win, great! When you don't, that's OK too! This circa-1870s Courthouse Steps quilt came with five other nineteenth-century antique quilts in a live auction textile lot—all in great condition, all won with one very low opening bid that was set and forgotten. Imagine my surprise when the winning bid email arrived in my in-box. Set your limit when bidding at auctions and stand fast. Sometimes you win bigger than imagined! ~Leah

waltz no. 2

FINISHED QUILT
60" × 68½"
FINISHED BLOCK
8½" × 8½"

Whirling and twirling, colorful prints waltz around the quilt, creating a pleasing secondary design. Careful color placement with contrasting values is key for creating the shadow effect and medallion look. Easy to piece, these straight-set blocks give a complicated look for a quilt that is big on appeal.

materials

Yardage is based on 42"-wide fabric.

¾ yard of red print #1 for blocks

⅜ yard of red print #2 for blocks

1⅜ yards of blue print #1 for blocks

⅝ yard of blue print #2 for blocks

⅜ yard of white print for blocks

⅞ yard of gray print for blocks

1⅜ yards of black print for blocks

¼ yard of indigo print #1 for blocks

⅞ yard of indigo print #2 for blocks

1⅛ yards of gold print #1 for blocks

¾ yard of gold print #2 for blocks

½ yard of black check for binding

3¾ yards of fabric for backing

66" × 75" piece of batting

cutting

All measurements include ¼"-wide seam allowances.

From red print #1, cut:
- 5 strips, 3" × 42"; crosscut into 60 squares, 3" × 3". Cut each square in half diagonally to yield 120 triangles.
- 4 strips, 2" × 42"

From red print #2, cut:
- 4 strips, 3" × 42"; crosscut into 52 squares, 3" × 3". Cut each square in half diagonally to yield 104 triangles.

From blue print #1, cut:
- 22 strips, 2" × 42"

From blue print #2, cut:
- 6 strips, 3" × 42"; crosscut into 68 squares, 3" × 3". Cut each square in half diagonally to yield 136 triangles.

Continued on page 81

Continued from page 79

From the white print, cut:
- 4 strips, 3" × 42"; crosscut into 44 squares, 3" × 3". Cut each square in half diagonally to yield 88 triangles.

From the gray print, cut:
- 2 strips, 5¾" × 42"; crosscut into 12 squares, 5¾" × 5¾". Cut each square into quarters diagonally to yield 48 triangles.
- 9 strips, 1⅜" × 42"

From the black print, cut:
- 3 strips, 5¾" × 42"; crosscut into 18 squares, 5¾" × 5¾". Cut each square into quarters diagonally to yield 72 triangles.
- 17 strips, 1⅜" × 42"

From indigo print #1, cut:
- 1 strip, 5¾" × 42"; crosscut into 4 squares, 5¾" × 5¾". Cut each square into quarters diagonally to yield 16 triangles.

From indigo print #2, cut:
- 4 strips, 5¾" × 42"; crosscut into 22 squares, 5¾" × 5¾". Cut each square into quarters diagonally to yield 88 triangles.
- 2 strips, 1⅜" × 42"

From gold print #1, cut:
- 18 strips, 2" × 42"

From gold print #2, cut:
- 12 strips, 2" × 42"

From the black check, cut:
- 7 strips, 2" × 42"

MAKING THE PINWHEEL UNITS

1 Join one red #1 and one blue #2 triangle along their long edges to make a half-square-triangle unit measuring 2⅝" square, including seam allowances. Make 48 A units.

Unit A.
Make 48 units,
2⅝" × 2⅝".

2 Repeat step 1 using the remaining red #1 and 72 white triangles to make 72 B units. Use the remaining blue #2 and 88 red #2 triangles to make 88 C units. Use the remaining red #2 and white triangles to make 16 D units.

Unit B.	Unit C.	Unit D.
Make 72 units,	Make 88 units,	Make 16 units,
2⅝" × 2⅝".	2⅝" × 2⅝".	2⅝" × 2⅝".

3 Lay out four A half-square-triangle units in two rows. Sew the units together into rows. Join the rows to make a pinwheel unit measuring 4¾" square, including seam allowances. Make 12 A units. In the same way, use the B units to make 18 of pinwheel unit B. Use the C units to make 22 of pinwheel unit C. Use the D units to make four of pinwheel unit D.

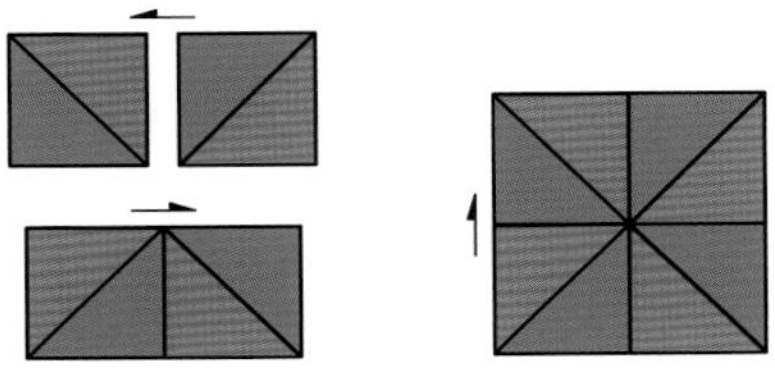

Unit A.
Make 12 units,
4¾" × 4¾".

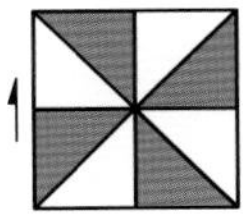

Unit B.	Unit C.	Unit D.
Make 18 units,	Make 22 units,	Make 4 units,
4¾" × 4¾".	4¾" × 4¾".	4¾" × 4¾".

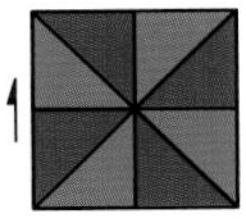

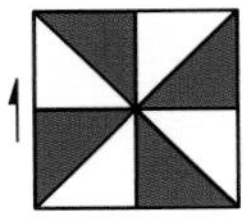

CONTRASTING VALUES

To create a shadow effect, choose different values of the same color, such as black and light gray. Placing the different values adjacent to each other in a quilt will give the illusion of a shadow.

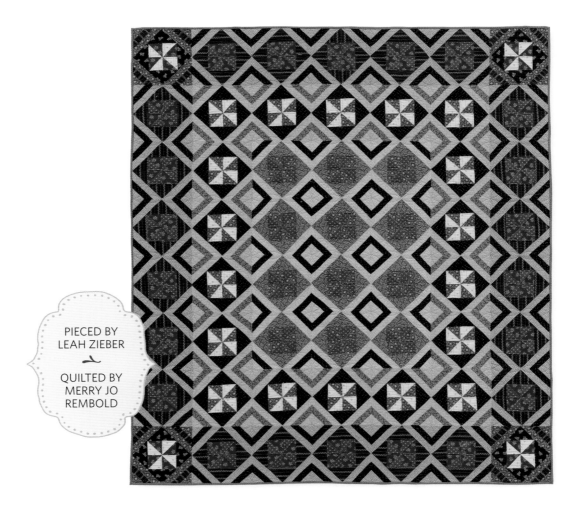

PIECED BY
LEAH ZIEBER

QUILTED BY
MERRY JO
REMBOLD

MAKING THE BLOCKS

1 Sew gray triangles to opposite sides of one A pinwheel unit. Sew gray triangles to the remaining two sides of the unit to make a center unit. Trim the unit to measure 6½" square, including seam allowances. Make 12 of center unit A.

2 In the same way, sew black triangles to each of the B pinwheel units to make 18 of center unit B. Sew indigo #2 triangles to each of the C pinwheel units to make 22 of center unit C. Sew indigo #1 triangles to each of the D pinwheel units to make four of center unit D.

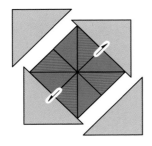 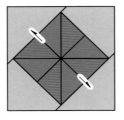

Unit A.
Make 12 units,
6½" × 6½".

Unit B.
Make 18 units,
6½" × 6½".

Unit C.
Make 22 units,
6½" × 6½".

Unit D.
Make 4 units,
6½" × 6½".

3 Join two gold #2 and one black 1⅜" strip along their long edges to make a strip set measuring 4⅜" × 42". Make six A strip sets. In the same way, join gold #1 and gray strips to make eight B strip sets. Join blue #1 and black strips to make 10 C strip sets. Join red #1 strips and indigo #2 strips to make two D strip sets.

Strip set A.
Make 6 strip sets, 4⅜" × 42".

Strip set B.
Make 9 strip sets, 4⅜" × 42".

Strip set C.
Make 11 strip sets, 4⅜" × 42".

Strip set D.
Make 2 strip sets, 4⅜" × 42".

TEMPLATE OR RULER?

You can use either a long quilting ruler or a template to cut the corner triangles from the strip sets. To use a ruler, align the 45° line with a seamline on the strip set. If you prefer to use a template, cut a 6" square from heavyweight template plastic. Then cut the square in half diagonally to make a triangle template. Align the long edge of the template with the outer edge of the strip set.

4 Using a rotary cutter and a ruler marked with a 45° line, trim one end of an A strip set at a 45° angle. Rotate the strip set, align the edge of the ruler with the newly cut edge, and line up the 45° line with a seamline. Cut along the edge of the ruler to release the triangle as shown. Continue in the same way to cut 48 A triangles. Repeat to cut 72 B triangles from the B strip sets, 88 C triangles from the C strip sets, and 16 D triangles from the D strip sets.

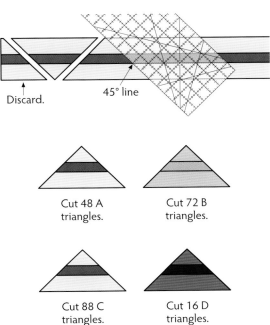

Cut 48 A triangles.

Cut 72 B triangles.

Cut 88 C triangles.

Cut 16 D triangles.

5 Trim off ½" from the long side of *each* triangle, making sure to keep like triangles together.

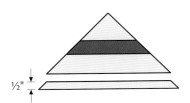

6 Sew A triangles to each side of an A center unit to make an A block measuring 9" square, including seam allowances. Make 12 A blocks. In the same way, join B triangles to the B center units to make 18 B blocks. Join C triangles to C center units to make 22 C blocks and D triangles to D center units to make four D blocks.

Block A.
Make 12 blocks,
9" × 9".

Block B.
Make 18 blocks,
9" × 9".

Block C.
Make 22 blocks,
9" × 9".

Block D.
Make 4 blocks,
9" × 9".

ASSEMBLING THE QUILT TOP

The blocks are assembled like a medallion center with two border units.

1 Lay out the A blocks in four rows of three blocks each as shown in the quilt assembly diagram on page 85. Sew the A blocks together into rows. Join the rows to make the quilt-top center. The quilt center should measure 26" × 34½", including seam allowances.

ASSEMBLY TIP

Pinning during quilt assembly is a must. Be sure to pin at every seam intersection. Taking this extra step ensures a seamless secondary design.

2 Join four B blocks to make a side border measuring 9" × 34½". Make two and sew them to opposite sides of the quilt center. Join five B blocks to make the top border measuring 9" × 43", including seam allowances. Repeat to make the bottom border. Sew these borders to the top and bottom of the quilt top. The quilt top should measure 43" × 51½", including seam allowances.

3 Join six C blocks to make a side border measuring 9" × 51½". Make two and sew them to opposite sides of the quilt center. Join five C blocks; add a D block to each end to make the top border measuring 9" × 60", including seam allowances. Repeat to make the bottom border. Sew these borders to the top and bottom of the quilt top. The quilt top should measure 60" × 68½".

FINISHING YOUR QUILT

For more information on finishing your quilt, visit ShopMartingale.com/HowtoQuilt.

1 Layer the quilt top, batting, and backing. Baste the layers together.

2 Quilt by hand or machine. Due to the many seams and secondary design, you may want to pick a simple quilting pattern that will show off the on-point squares in the quilt. The quilt shown is custom machine quilted using a simple loop design in the center and a complex fleur-de-lis design in the borders.

3 Use the black check 2"-wide strips to make the binding, and then attach the binding to the quilt. Using a narrow binding helps create an authentic antique look.

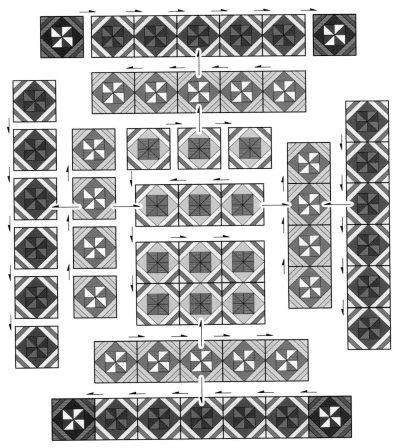

Quilt assembly

ANTIQUE INSPIRATION

Creating shadows and secondary designs may seem like a contemporary quiltmaking technique, but it's not new. In the late 19th century, one quiltmaker was using fabric colors and values to create this stunning circa-1890s quilt with its medallion setting and secondary design of concentric squares. The mourning prints in blacks and grays contrast against the double pinks and blue checks, helping to carry the eye across the unique design in this one-of-a-kind quilt.
~Leah

SCOTTISH Reel

FINISHED QUILT
67" × 67"
FINISHED BLOCK
9½" × 9½"

Like the colorful skirts at a country folk dance, Scottish Reel is sure to brighten any room. Cheery cheddar sashing anchored by green nine-patch cornerstones carries the eye between the vibrant blocks. For a larger quilt, try adding an outer border or two.

MateriaLS

Yardage is based on 42"-wide fabric.

¼ yard *each* of 25 assorted prints in green, rust, brown, and purple for blocks

⅜ yard of yellow print for side and corner blocks

2⅝ yards of shirting print A for blocks

⅜ yard of dark green print for sashing blocks

⅓ yard of shirting print B for sashing blocks

2 yards of cheddar print for sashing and binding

4¼ yards of fabric for backing

75" × 75" piece of batting

CUTTING

All measurements include ¼"-wide seam allowances.

From *each* of the 25 assorted prints, cut:
- 1 square, 4" × 4" (25 total)
- 4 squares, 3½" × 3½" (100 total)
- 4 rectangles, 2" × 4" (100 total)

From *each* of 10 assorted prints, cut:
- 1 square, 4" × 4" (10 total)
- 3 squares, 3½" × 3½" (30 total)
- 2 rectangles, 2" × 4" (20 total)

From the yellow print, cut:
- 2 strips, 3½" × 42"; crosscut into 14 squares, 3½" × 3½"
- 1 strip, 4" × 42"; crosscut into:
    8 rectangles, 2" × 4"
    6 squares, 4" × 4"

From shirting print A, cut:
- 29 strips, 2" × 42"; crosscut into 576 squares, 2" × 2"
- 7 strips, 4" × 42"; crosscut into 128 rectangles, 2" × 4"

From the dark green print, cut:
- 8 strips, 1¼" × 42"

From shirting print B, cut:
- 7 strips, 1¼" × 42"

From the cheddar print, cut:
- 5 strips, 10" × 42"; crosscut into 64 strips, 2¾" × 10"
- 7 strips, 2" × 42"

MAKING THE CENTER BLOCKS

Use ¼" seam allowances. Press seam allowances in the directions indicated by the arrows.

1 Draw a diagonal line from corner to corner on the wrong side of each shirting print A 2" square. Place marked squares on opposite corners of a print 3½" square, right sides together and corners aligned. Sew on the marked line. Trim the excess corner fabric, leaving a ¼" seam allowance. In the same way, sew marked squares on the two remaining corners of the square to make a corner unit measuring 3½" square, including seam allowances. Make a total of 130 corner units.

Make 130 units, 3½" × 3½".

2 Repeat step 1 to make 14 corner units using the remaining marked squares and yellow 3½" squares.

Make 14 units, 3½" × 3½".

3 Join a print rectangle to the long edge of a shirting print A rectangle to make a side unit measuring 3½" × 4", including seam allowances. Make 120 units.

Make 120 units, 3½" × 4".

4 Join a yellow rectangle to the long edge of a shirting print A rectangle to make a side unit measuring 3½" × 4", including seam allowances. Make eight units.

Make 8 units, 3½" × 4".

5 Lay out four corner units, four side units, and one 4" square, all matching, in three rows. Sew the units and square together into rows. Join the rows to make a block measuring 10" square, including seam allowances. Make 25 blocks.

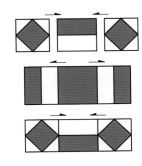 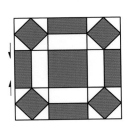

Make 25 blocks, 10" × 10".

MAKING THE SIDE AND CORNER BLOCKS

1 Lay out three corner units, two side units, and one 4" square, all matching, in three rows as shown. Sew the units together into rows. Join the rows.

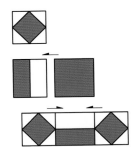 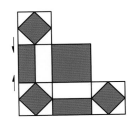

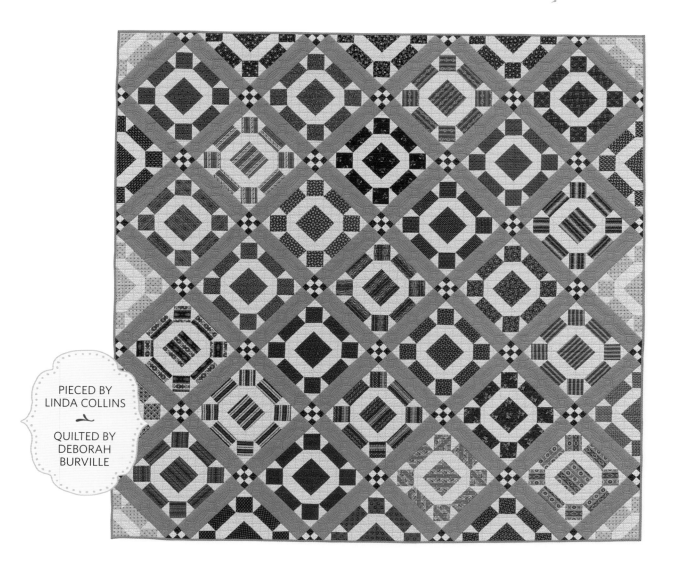

PIECED BY
LINDA COLLINS

QUILTED BY
DEBORAH
BURVILLE

2 On the wrong side of the unit, use a pencil and ruler to draw a diagonal line ¼" from the diagonal center. (Do not draw the center line.) Sew ⅛" from the pencil line as shown to stabilize the bias edge. Using a ruler and rotary cutter, cut on the drawn line to make a side block. Make 10 assorted print blocks and two yellow blocks.

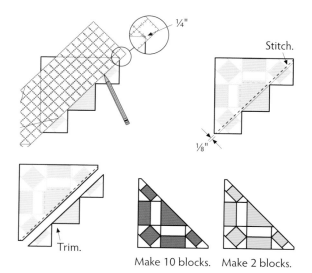

¼"

Stitch.

⅛"

Trim.

Make 10 blocks.   Make 2 blocks.

3 Lay out two yellow corner units, one yellow side unit, and one yellow 4" square as shown. Sew the units in the top row together, and then add the square to the bottom of the joined row.

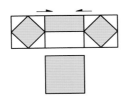
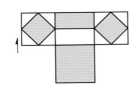

4 On the wrong side of the unit, use a pencil and ruler to draw a diagonal line in each direction ¼" from the diagonal center. (Do not draw the center line.) Sew ⅛" from the drawn lines as shown to stabilize bias edges. Using a ruler and rotary cutter, cut on the drawn lines. Make four corner blocks.

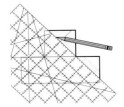
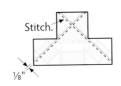

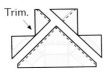

Make 4 corner blocks.

MAKING THE SASHING BLOCKS

1 Join two dark green strips and one shirting B strip along their long edges to make a strip set measuring 2¾" × 42", including seam allowances. Make three strip sets. Cut the strip sets into 80 A segments, 1¼" × 2¾".

1¼"

Strip set A.
Make 3 strip sets, 2¾" × 42".
Cut 80 segments, 1¼" × 2¾".

2 Join two shirting B strips and one dark green strip along their long edges to make a strip set measuring 2¾" × 42", including seam allowances. Make two strip sets. Cut the strip sets into 40 B segments, 1¼" × 2¾".

1¼"

Strip set B.
Make 2 strip sets, 2¾" × 42".
Cut 40 segments, 1¼" × 2¾".

3 Join two A segments and one B segment to make a Nine Patch block measuring 2¾" square, including seam allowances. Make 40 blocks.

Make 40 blocks,
2¾" × 2¾".

4 On the wrong side of 16 blocks, use a pencil and ruler to draw a diagonal line ¼" from the diagonal center. (Do not draw the center line.) Sew ⅛" from the marked line as shown to stabilize the bias edges. Using a ruler and rotary cutter, cut on the marked line. Make 16 half blocks.

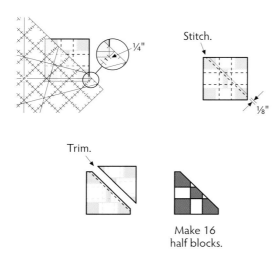

Stitch.

¼"

⅛"

Trim.

Make 16 half blocks.

ASSEMBLING THE QUILT TOP

Lay out the center blocks, cheddar strips, and sashing blocks in diagonal rows as shown in the quilt assembly diagram below. Add the side, corner, and sashing half blocks around the perimeter. Sew the blocks and cheddar strips together into rows. Join the rows, adding the corner triangles last, to complete the quilt top, which should measure 67" square.

FINISHING THE QUILT

For more information on finishing your quilt, visit ShopMartingale.com/HowtoQuilt.

1 Layer the quilt top, batting, and backing. Baste the layers together.

2 Quilt by hand or machine. The quilt shown is custom machine quilted with cross-hatching in the blocks and darts in the sashing.

3 Use the cheddar 2"-wide strips to make the binding, and then attach the binding to the quilt. Using a narrow binding helps create an authentic antique look.

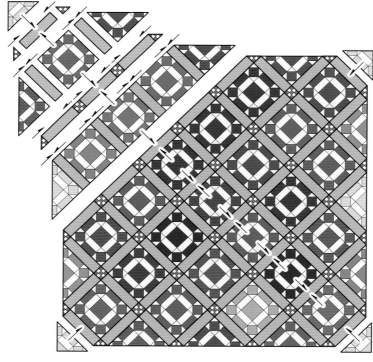

Quilt assembly

ANTIQUE INSPIRATION

Despite popular belief, not all 19th century quilts are brown, and this circa 1880s Rolling Stone quilt is evidence of that The cheddar sashing and nine-patch cornerstones establish a foundation for the blocks that is quite striking. By keeping the quilting simple inside the block, with only crosshatching, the colors are allowed to become the focus of the quilt. Purchased at Houston International Quilt Festival, this eye-catcher has remained a longtime favorite from my collection. ~Linda

about the authors

LINDA COLLINS
of Wonga Park, Victoria, AU

Quilting has been a part of my life for over 30 years. I made my first quilt for my second-born child some 30-odd years ago. I have been collecting and studying antique quilts for over 20 years. The past 10 years I've been publishing patterns based on my antique quilts in Australian and international magazines. Sharing my antique-quilt collection through trunk shows and redesigning quilts from them are both passions that are at the very core of my being. My wish is that you are inspired to make a quilt from the quilts Leah and I have shared in our book. I love what I do and love inspiring other quilters to reproduce antique quilts. Quiltmaking and collecting have been an adventure through which I have made many wonderful friendships around the world.

Born and raised in Australia, I learned to knit at the age of eight, and to this day, whenever I find knitting needles in my hand, the memories of my beloved grandmother are quite strong.

I've been a wife of 40 years to Paul; mum to three, Becci, John, and Braedon; mum-in-law to son-in-law Graham and daughters-in-law Lauren and Kara; and proud grandma to Laila and Michael. Cooking is another of my passions, and nothing makes me happier than preparing a feast for family and friends to share as they gather around my kitchen table. When not traveling the world visiting friends, quilt exhibits, or museums, I divide my time between my home in Wonga Park, Victoria, and my beach house. These landscapes provide peace and inspiration aplenty.

Leah Zieber

of Temecula, California, USA

I have been working independently with collectors and quilt historians for 20 years, cataloging and researching American quilts and textiles. I love to share my own collection of antique quilts and textiles and my knowledge of American quilts with guilds throughout the United States and abroad through lectures, workshops, and quilt-history retreats.

My antique-reproduction quilts have won awards and been displayed in museums and historical homes across the country as well as published by American Quilt Study Group. With a love for stories of quilt people and my passion for quilting, I enjoy bringing the past to life for other quilters through the American Heritage Quilt series of historical fiction I write and the reproduction-quilt patterns I design. You can connect with me on Facebook, Instagram, Etsy, and my web page, zieberquilts.com.

acknowledgments

Special thanks are due to the many people who've helped make the dream of writing this book a reality.

LINDA WOULD LIKE TO THANK:

- **Martingale,** and its staff, without whom there would not be this book. Thank you for your trust in us. Your team has brought our dream to life within the pages of this book.

- **Robyn Ahern,** heartfelt thanks for so willingly taking on the challenge of making the only hand-pieced quilt in this book, and knocking it out of the park.

- **Paula Cochran,** for all the hand-holding, technical training, and maintaining my sanity when computer issues arose. More heartfelt thanks than you can know.

- **My quilty friends,** near and far. Your support and encouragement always warm my heart. YOU inspire me! Thank you!

- **My gorgeous machine quilters, Debbie Burville and Katrina Wilson,** each with your very own magic.

- **Leah Zieber,** thank you for the journey that we have shared. The memories will remain with me forever: the rambling emails, the all-hour chats from across the pond, the enthusiasm you inspire in me. I was truly blessed the day I met you.

- **My beautiful blessings, Becci and Graham, John and Lauren, Braedon and Kara,** the joy you all give me is exceeded only by the love I have for Laila and Michael.

- **The greatest of my blessings, my dearest husband, Paul,** your support has allowed me to follow my dream and you're always ready and willing to take on even the craziest of my ideas. I love you!

LEAH WOULD LIKE TO THANK:

- **Martingale,** for the opportunity to share my passion for antique quilts with other quiltmakers and collectors. This really is a dream come true.

- **Pat L. Nickols,** thank you for a solid foundation. I'm blessed by the continued opportunities to learn about textile history with you.

- **Susan Greene,** thanks for your generous help and support, my friend. Can't wait for the next road trip!

- **Savannah Pfautz,** you always lift me up higher than I can ever see going on my own. Together we climb mountains!

- **Merry Jo Rembold,** your machine quilting makes my quilts shine! Bless you.

- **Paula Cochran,** you saved my life one night! Thank you.

- **Linda Collins,** here's to a friendship that spans great distances and time, and still remains true. I look forward to the future with anticipation of what we can achieve.

- **Alan, Kindra, Jonathan, Rebecca, and Katherine,** mothers give life, children offer mothers great purpose. Thank you, my children, for always giving my life great purpose.

- **Gary Zieber,** you keep me grounded. Without you, nothing makes sense. Thank you for always encouraging me to be a better person. I love you!